HERE I COME, READY OR NOT

MORRIS L. VENDEN

Pacific Press Publishing Association
Boise, Idaho
Oshawa, Ontario, Canada

Edited by Don Mansell
Designed by Tim Larson
Cover photo by Duane Tank
Type set in 10/12 Century Schoolbook

Copyright ©1987 by
Pacific Press Publishing Association
Printed in United States of America
All rights reserved

Library of Congress Catalog Card number: 87-72909

The author assumes full responsibility for the accuracy of all facts and quotations cited in this book.

ISBN 0-8163-0733-4

87 88 89 90 91 • 5 4 3 2 1

Contents

Foreword

Ever since the exit from Eden, mankind has had the Promise. Jesus is coming! It has been the hope, the encouragement, the inspiration for God's people in all ages. And yes, it has finally become almost an embarrassment, for we were told a long time ago that He would have come a long time ago, had we been faithful. We weren't and He didn't. We are still here.

The Promise states that He is coming "soon." But when "soon" lingers for centuries, we who are limited to three score years and ten find it hard to understand the term. And the Promise of His return has been turned into a kind of threat for some; the time of trouble has been used as a sort of vegetarian hellfire. As a result, the second advent has often ended up as little more than the perpetual cry of "Wolf, wolf."

Certain things are to take place before Jesus can come. The gospel is to go to all the world. The church is to fully reflect His image. But as we consider the population explosion as compared to the growth of the church, and as we judge the spiritual condition of those around us, we relax. It looks like it's going to be a long, hard winter! Yet there is always a fear that we might have missed something, particularly when we see the smoke beginning to rise, and so we make our detailed charts and timetables. Far too many church members have watched and studied last-day events for the purpose of trying to catch the last trolley out.

It is said that President Harding, who had Adventist relatives, used to say that when Turkey was driven from Europe (a sure sign that probation was about to close), he would join the church. He died before he ever joined. Far too few of God's children have lived so close to Him that it would not matter whether He should come immediately, or ten thousand years in the future.

Yet the Promise still stands. He's coming. The signs of His soon return are reaching fulfillment, one by one. It has happened slower than we had hoped, or feared. But we are no longer having to depend upon the moon and the stars to argue our case. Thinking people everywhere see a world that is headed for suicide.

Within the church, the rising emphasis upon salvation by faith in Jesus Christ alone has resulted in the shaking we were told about. We see people going one way or the other—and fast. Churches, institutions, and families are being split apart, as the lifting up of Jesus brings decision.

And the questions are being asked with increasing frequency. What place does the subject of last-day events have in the great theme of righteousness by faith? Do we perhaps need a fresh look at topics like the time of trouble, the final destruction of the wicked, the national Sunday law? Is there more that might be discovered in these traditional Adventist understandings, if they were viewed through "relationship" glasses, instead of with the "behavioral" focus? In the final crisis, will there be security for the one who has made the daily fellowship and communion with God his top priority? Or do we also need to work hard to develop enough self-control to make it through the time without an Intercessor? Does the truth of salvation through faith alone bring enough assurance and power to take us through the times ahead?

What if Jesus were to come this year? Would that be good

news, or bad news? Do you think you would be ready to meet Him? Or does the thought of an immediate, actual, visible second coming of Christ make you uncomfortable? What would be your reaction if you heard His voice today, echoing from the gates of heaven to His waiting church, "Here I come, ready or not!"

Chapter 1
The Coming Crisis

One day my brother and I were playing out by the woodshed at Grandma's house. He was six years old, and I was four. He was stung by a yellow jacket and began to scream and cry and jump up and down. I got after him for being such a sissy, until the yellow jacket's brother stung me—and that was the first duet my brother and I ever sang!

It's easy to be brave before the crisis comes—but it is when the crisis comes that we see ourselves as we really are.

There's no point in taking up sky diving if you're afraid to jump off the back steps. Don't bother to set out to cross the seven seas if you get seasick in the bathtub. It's hopeless to register for college trig if you never learned what six times nine equals. Jeremiah says it this way: "If thou hast run with the footmen, and they have wearied thee, then how canst thou contend with horses? and if in the land of peace, wherein thou trustedst, they wearied thee, then how wilt thou do in the swelling of Jordan?" Jeremiah 12:5.

Jesus told a parable about crises. It's a short one, found in Matthew 7:24-27. "Whosoever heareth these sayings of mine, and doeth them, I will liken him unto a wise man, which built his house upon a rock: and the rain descended, and the floods came, and the winds blew, and beat upon that house; and it fell not: for it was founded upon a rock. And every one that heareth these sayings of mine, and doeth them not, shall be likened unto a foolish man which built his house upon the sand: and the rain descended, and the floods came, and the winds blew, and beat upon that house; and it fell: and great was the fall of it."

Do you remember singing about the wise man and the foolish man when you were in kindergarten? "The wise man built his house upon the rock." It was a good song, wasn't it! But there is one major lesson in the story of the wise man and the foolish man that we want particularly to notice. When the storm comes, the house does not change foundations. That's a heavy-duty point. When the crisis comes in your life, you do not change foundations. The crisis only reveals upon what foundation you have already built.

Therefore, it is the love of God that allows the small winds to blow against us to show us our true condition, so that we can prepare for the big winds that are to come before it's all over. Since a crisis doesn't move us over to the right foundation, our only hope is that the little crises will help us realize our need and that as a result we find the grace to change afterward; for when the angels release the final winds of strife in this world, it will be too late for anyone to change foundations. Our fate will have already been decided.

There's something else we can learn from a crisis. Not only does it reveal the direction in which you were already going, but it will usually increase your momentum.

The apostle Peter said, "I will never deny You."

Jesus said, "You will deny Me this very night." And not only did Peter deny Jesus, but when the crisis came, he added cursing and swearing to it as well. The crisis increased his momentum in the direction he was already going.

For Simon the Cyrene, who was willing to speak up in behalf of Jesus on the road to Calvary, the crisis of being forced to carry His cross caused him to go farther in the direction he was headed. It works both ways. When you're climbing a mountain and you fall down, after you get up again you are usually a step or two ahead of where you fell. But when you are going down the mountain and fall, you usually end up several steps below where you were when you fell. That's the way it works in everyday crises as well as in the great crisis ahead.

So, even though a crisis does not change us, and even though it often increases the momentum in the direction in which we were already going, it is possible to ponder and think and change the direction after the minor crisis—if there is still time. That's why it is an evidence of God's love that He allows the small winds to blow, to open our eyes to our direction before the big winds come upon us. He allows us to be tested by the footmen, so that we'll know how we are going to do with the horses. Can you appreciate that kind of love?

Sometimes the small winds seem pretty strong! One day I toured the Outward Bound school in the Rocky Mountains with some friends. At the end of the course was a tall tree, and we were expected to bail out into a net below. My friends thought I had decided to spend the rest of my life in that tree before I finally found the courage to let loose—and discovered that it wasn't nearly as bad as I had anticipated.

But the times ahead of us, at the close of this earth's history, are of a different nature. You can read about it in *The Great Controversy,* page 622. "It is often the case that trouble is greater in anticipation than in reality; but this is not true of the crisis before us. The most vivid presentation cannot reach the magnitude of the ordeal." There will be no safety for anyone, except for those who know the secret place of the Most High and abide under the shadow of the Almighty. And those who are delivered will be the ones who have found that secret place under His shadow *before* the crisis comes.

My father wanted my brother and me to learn to play the piano, and so he offered to pay us 10 cents an hour to practice. (My conscience still bothers me over some of the hours I turned in for my 10 cents!) But it is impossible to make it to the concert stage at 10 cents an hour for practicing! In fact, it was a wonder we learned anything at all. But I learned to play a song that my dad liked to sing, and so he would take me with him on Sabbath out to a place called Otter Lake in Michigan, one of those little churches that meets on Sabbath afternoon. He would get up and sing the one song I knew, while I accompanied him.

In that little church was a woman whose husband couldn't have cared less about religion. In fact, he was actually hostile. He hated the church, and he hated preachers. I remember my father trying to stop and visit with him on several occasions, and when my father would knock at the front door, the man would sneak out the back door.

Well, this woman had a burden for her husband, and she continued to pray. Then one night, in the middle of the Michigan winter, the phone rang at our place. My father got up to answer the phone and learned that this man was asking for a preacher. So he went out into the deep snow and slipped and slid his way to Otter Lake.

He described it later, telling us of how he had walked into the house to find this man had suffered a major heart attack. The pain was so severe that he couldn't sit up, and he couldn't lie down. He was propped up in a half-way position, gasping, and trying to keep from screaming. And as my father walked in, the man looked at him and said, "Preacher, if you can do anything for this poor man, do it, and do it quick!"

My father told about the strange, helpless feeling that came over him as he realized that here was someone who barely had enough blood pumping across his brain to keep him conscious—let alone think clearly enough to make a decision concerning eternal issues.

If a person doesn't respond to the love of Jesus before the pressure of a crisis, what is there about panic that would enable him to respond more fully to the love of Jesus then? Perhaps there have been some genuine deathbed repentances. But careful examination will probably reveal that there has been a lot of forethought involved that wasn't apparent to those watching. We know God can do the impossible, and we're thankful for that. But as we consider the last-day events and the final crisis in this world, what a challenge it is to do our thinking and deciding now, before it is too late, because we are told that when the final crisis hits, there are going to be many people unprepared. You can read about it in Amos 8:11, 12. "Behold, the days come, saith the Lord God, that I will send a famine in the land, not a famine of bread, nor a thirst for water, but of hearing the words of the Lord: and they shall wander from sea to sea, and from the north even to the east, they shall run to and fro to seek the word of the Lord, and shall not find it."

How can you know you are ready for the great crisis that is to come upon this world? How can you know that your house stands on the right foundation, before the winds blow?

The key is found in the same chapter of Matthew, in the verses just preceding the parable of the wise and foolish men. Matthew 7:22, 23: "Many will say to me in that day, Lord, Lord, have we not prophesied in thy name? and in thy name have cast out devils? and in thy name done many wonderful works? And then will I profess unto them, I never knew you: depart from me, ye that work iniquity."

Who are these people that work iniquity? They have cast out devils—so exorcism isn't going to prove anything. They have prophesied—so prophesying doesn't prove anything. And they have done many wonderful works—but that doesn't prove anything either!

Jesus says to them, "I don't know you." The religion of Jesus Christ is a very personal affair. He knocks at the door for the purpose of coming in and sitting down and eating with us. Eating is one of the most intimate things you do. You eat with your family, with your friends, with those you are close to. It is a time for fellowship and communication.

So the crucial question is, Do you know Jesus? The same

issue was involved in the story of the ten bridesmaids, found in Matthew 25. They all thought they were ready for the coming of the bridegroom. But there was a crisis of waiting. The wise were prepared for a long wait. The foolish were not. And the crisis of having to wait revealed that only five of the bridesmaids were really ready for the wedding.

When at last the cry was made, "Behold, the bridegroom cometh; go ye out to meet him," the wise had oil with which to trim their lamps. They met the bridegroom when he came and went in to the wedding.

But the foolish had no oil left. Verses 8 and 9 of Matthew 25 tell us, "The foolish said unto the wise, Give us of your oil; for our lamps are gone out. But the wise answered, saying, Not so; lest there be not enough for us and you: but go ye rather to them that sell, and buy for yourselves."

One of the lessons of this parable is that personal experience is not transferrable. At first glance, it might sound like the wise were being stingy. But they weren't being stingy; they were only facing reality. Nobody's experience is good enough for somebody else. Nobody slides into heaven on the coattails of another, whether it's father or mother, son or daughter, prophet or priest or king. God has no grandsons, only sons and daughters.

You know the rest of the story. While the foolish virgins were rushing about, trying to obtain that which they lacked, the bridegroom came. Those who were ready went in with him to the marriage, and *the door was shut!*

Afterward the foolish knocked at the door, and they said, Open the door! But the answer was given, "I know you not."

Do you know Jesus? Are you spending time day by day in becoming acquainted with Him? It is through the personal fellowship and communion with Him that you come to know Him as your Friend. And it is through knowing Him that you are ready to meet Him when He comes again.

Chapter 2
How to Be Ready

Have you ever heard the story of the schoolboy who kept the messiest desk in his classroom? It's the sort of story that shows up in books of 500 sermon illustrations! This boy just couldn't seem to keep his desk in order. It was always overflowing with books and papers and pens.

One day the superintendent of schools came to the classroom to announce a contest. He told the students that he would return, at some time in the future, without being announced ahead of time. When he returned, he would inspect the desks, and the student whose desk was neatest and most orderly would receive a prize.

The boy with the messy desk was immediately interested. After the superintendent went on his way, the boy said, "I am going to try to win that prize!"

The other students laughed. "Why, you don't have a chance," they exclaimed. "How could you possibly have the neatest desk in the room?"

"I will clean my desk every Friday afternoon," the boy decided. "Then it will be clean to start each week, and I will surely win the prize."

"But what if the superintendent comes on Thursday?" asked the other students.

The boy thought for a minute. "Then I will clean my desk every single morning," he declared.

"But what if the superintendent comes to inspect our desks in the afternoon, just before time to go home?" they asked him.

He hesitated, remembering how quickly his desk got out of order, even after it had been cleaned. Finally he said, "I will *keep* it clean, so that no matter when the superintendent comes, I will be ready."

The conclusion to this story escapes me! Perhaps it was left open-ended on purpose. Or perhaps the boy kept his desk clean and won the prize and went on to become General Conference president! I don't know. But it serves to illustrate the point that we want to notice here, that there is something more important than getting ready for Jesus to come. It is *being* ready. In fact, there is no such thing as getting ready! The challenge is to be ready and to stay ready.

Being ready and staying ready can present us with a real challenge. Getting ready would be much easier!

When some of your friends or relatives call you on the phone and make arrangements to come for a visit, you have the opportunity to get ready. They tell you they expect to arrive on such and such a day. They may even know ahead of time exactly when they will reach your house. And so you have the chance to get ready.

But have you ever lived in a house that was up for sale? It's like having perpetual guests! If there is any day of the week when you get up late and don't take time to make the bed or leave the breakfast dishes in the sink, that's sure to be the day that someone comes to see the house.

And while your houseguests might be polite enough to stay in the living room or guest rooms unless you invite them elsewhere, prospective buyers are notorious for having no respect for your privacy! They not only go right into your bedroom or study—they'll open closets and cupboards as well—and even insist on seeing the inside of the garage!

Jesus told a parable in Luke 12 about a servant left in charge of his master's affairs. Then He told of two possible endings to the story, leaving the hearers to decide the outcome for themselves. Either the servant would be ready and would be found faithful when his lord returned—or he would say in his heart, "My lord delayeth his coming" (verse 45), and put off getting ready for some future time. For the second servant, the return of his lord would be bad news—just as the coming of the bridegroom was bad news for the five bridesmaids who were unprepared. And the challenge given to them is our challenge as well, "Watch therefore, for ye know neither the day nor the hour wherein the Son of man cometh." Matthew 25:13.

But this presents us with a problem. Because of the fact that behaviorism is so deeply engrained in the human heart, it is easy to look at the issues of getting ready or staying ready or being ready in terms of behavior. It's easy to say, "Let's see: What will *I* need to *do* to be ready?"

Here's where the discussions about perfection begin—and continue until midnight. How perfect is perfect? How perfect do we have to be to be perfect enough? For how long do we have to be perfect before Christ comes again in order for it to count?

Perhaps here is where some of the interest in the charts and timetables and order of last-day events rises to the top. Being a perfect Christian can be hard work, just as being a perfect housekeeper can be hard work.

Some of us may try to find out when the deadline is, so that we can rein up our willpower and force ourselves to be perfect just long enough to make it under the wire. We know how hard it is to be perfect, and so we conclude that our only hope is to try to be perfect for the shortest possible time!

It has been said that it's hard to have houseguests who stay to visit for more than just a few days, because it's hard to be nicer than you really are for more than a short time. And perhaps it is this element of human nature that keeps us looking for the last trolley out when it comes to the end of the world and the return of Christ.

So let me ask you a question. If we could prove that it is absolutely essential that you become perfect in order to be ready for the last-day events, what difference would that make in your life today? Or if we could prove that it is unnecessary (or perhaps impossible!) for you to become perfect before the end of time, what difference would *that* make in your life today?

The story is told of Francis of Assisi, who was out hoeing in his garden one day, and someone came along and said, "Hey, Francis! If you knew that you were going to die tonight, what would you do?"

He replied, "I'd finish hoeing my garden."

Do you give St. Francis good marks or bad marks for getting his garden hoed? Was he exhibiting assurance—or arrogance? Was he wise—or naive?

One thing is certain: if being ready for the end of time is based upon anything *we* can do, in terms of behavior, then our attention will be inevitably focused upon ourselves and our own performance. And at any time we look to ourselves, we lose sight of Jesus and His power.

But think for a moment of being ready and staying ready from the standpoint of relationship. If we are in fellowship and communication with Jesus day by day, then the pressure is off. Our part in the preparation takes place when we make that decision each morning to give God top priority in the day—to spend time in communion with Him. If we have made the decision to take time to seek Him morning by morning until He comes again, then we will be in daily relationship with Him, and eternal life will already be ours.

Does that sound too simple? Read 1 John 5:11, 12. "This is the record, that God hath given to us eternal life, and this life is in his Son. He that hath the Son hath life; and he that hath not the Son of God hath not life." What does it mean to "have the Son"? We use the same terminology in describing our human relationships. We say, "I have a friend. I have a wife. You have a husband." What are we saying? That we have a relationship with someone.

Eternal life doesn't begin in eternity—it begins here and now, as we enter into fellowship with Christ. Jesus said it in John 6:54. "Whoso eateth my flesh, and drinketh my blood, *hath* eternal life." (Emphasis supplied.) It doesn't say, "shall have eternal life," or "will have eternal life," or "might have eternal life." It says that the one who enters into the close fellowship with Christ that is represented by eating His flesh and drinking His blood *has* eternal life. And Jesus explains it a little more clearly in verse 63 of the same chapter, "The words that I speak unto you, they are spirit, and they are life." So it is by partaking of His Word, the Bread of Life, that we accept eternal life.

When we look at eternal life with relationship glasses, instead of with behavior glasses, it becomes apparent that eternal life is something we can have—not merely something we can hope for. If we really believe this and are committed to seeking the day-by-day relationship with Christ, then our attention will be upon Him and His love, and His sacrifice in our behalf, and we will trust Him to accomplish *for* us whatever is necessary in terms of changed lives and victory and perfection and all the rest of it.

If you already have the gift of eternal life, then you are ready for the coming of Jesus. If Jesus is living His life in you, He will work in you to do His will—and obedience and victory and overcoming, yes, and even perfection, will be the ultimate results.

Are you afraid that the relationship with Christ won't be enough? Are you worried that you need to help God out, to add your willpower and backbone and grit and determination to His power for you? Look again at the famous passage in *The Desire of Ages,* page 668. "All true obedience comes from the heart. It was heart work with Christ. And if we consent, He will so identify Himself with our thoughts and aims, so blend our hearts and minds into conformity to His will, that when obeying Him we shall be but carrying out our own impulses. The will, refined and sanctified, will find its highest delight in doing His service. When we know God as it is our privilege to know Him, our life will be a life of continual obedience. Through an appreciation of the character of Christ, through communion with God, sin will become hateful to us."

Add to that one more sentence, from the same book, page 302. "If the eye is kept fixed on Christ, the work of the Spirit ceases not until the soul is conformed to His image."

Now let me ask you something. If you come to the place of being in such close fellowship with Christ that when obeying Him you are carrying out your own impulses, if you find your highest delight in doing His service, if your life is a life of continual obedience, if sin has become hateful to you, and if your soul is conformed to His image, then do you think you would be obedient?

If we look to ourselves and how we are doing, there's not a chance in the world that we can be saved. But if we look to Jesus and keep our eyes fixed upon Him, there's not a chance in the world that we will be lost.

Being ready and staying ready involves the ongoing relationship with Christ. "This is life eternal, that they might know thee the only true God, and Jesus Christ, whom thou hast sent." John 17:3. Do you know Him today? Did you commit your life to Him anew today and accept once again His grace? If you are ready to meet Him today, and if you continue to be ready each day as it comes, you will be ready in that final day for His return.

Chapter 3
Why the Delay?

"Like the stars in the vast circuit of their appointed path, God's purposes know no haste and no delay."—*The Desire of Ages,* p. 32. How's that for a place to start! Why the delay? *There has been no delay!* And perhaps we could end this chapter right here.

But it certainly appears that there has been a delay, doesn't it? We've been expecting the second coming of Christ for quite a few years now. When gunpowder was invented, people said, "That's it. That's the end of the world." And we've had a lot of water under the bridge since the invention of gunpowder. When the first atom bomb exploded, we said, "There it is—only seconds to midnight!" But atom bombs have been around for a long time now. With every crisis or disaster, someone is sure to say, "This must be the end." Yet we are still here, still waiting for the return of Christ. To our human understanding, there has been a long delay. And we wonder at times if the fulfillment of the Promise will ever come.

As good Adventists, we have spent our share of time in studying and hearing about last-day events. The emphasis upon the soon return of Christ has been always present. It might be easy to decide to hoe the garden with St. Francis, as we noticed in the previous chapter, and decide that the study of eschatology is no longer relevant. After all, if prep-

21

aration for the coming of Christ is based upon relationship with Him, and if we should live so that it makes no difference whether He comes today or 10,000 years from today, then what is the value of time spent in studying and discussing the details? Why not just let it happen?

One reason for studying the prophecies and promises regarding last-day events is to be found in John 13:19. Jesus was speaking to His disciples and said, "Now I tell you before it come, that, when it is come to pass, ye may believe." God wants us to know a certain amount about what is coming so that we can be assured that He is in control. He is not caught by surprise when a crisis or trouble comes. And when He lets us know in advance what to expect, when the events occur just as He told us, we are affirmed in our belief in Him. That's a good reason right there, isn't it?

There's another reason to study about the end of the world and the signs of Christ's coming. It's found in *Steps to Christ*, pages 21 and 22. "The exceeding rewards for right-doing, the enjoyment of heaven, the society of the angels, the communion and love of God and His Son, the elevation and extension of all our powers throughout eternal ages—are these not mighty incentives and encouragements to urge us to give the heart's loving service to our Creator and Redeemer? And, on the other hand, the judgments of God pronounced against sin, the inevitable retribution, the degradation of our character, and the final destruction, are presented in God's Word to warn us against the service of Satan." So God does use the incentives of a heaven to win and a hell to shun to startle people, to gain their attention, so that they will recognize their need of His salvation.

It would be too bad to continue forever with a heaven to win and a hell to shun as the only motives for seeking God. But God will take us wherever He can get us, and as we continue to come to Him, He can then lead us to the greater motives of seeking Him for His own sake. As we see His love for us and gain a greater understanding of His character, our love for Him will grow. The time will come when we can join with the songwriter who said:

If walls there weren't jasper
And streets were not gold
If mansions would crumble
And if folks there still grew old,
Still I'd see everything I've been longing to see
Jesus will be what makes it heaven for me.

So to know what is coming ahead of time, so that when it happens our trust in God is strengthened, and to realize that we have a heaven to win and a hell to shun are both legitimate reasons for studying about last-day events. And there is one more reason that we could notice as well. That is the reason of anticipation! Particularly when there seems to have been a long delay, the Promise is needed to reassure us. For the one who is a friend of God, the Promise of His coming is wonderful news! The joy of anticipation can keep our courage high, in spite of the roughness of the road.

It is nice sometimes to be surprised! But when someone who is dear to you is coming to town, part of the joy of the visit is in being able to look forward to his coming and prepare especially for the time together.

Would it be possible to look forward to the coming of Christ with the same sort of expectation? Could we study the charts and timetables and signs because we can hardly wait for Him to come—rather than with dread or fear that He will arrive before we are ready for Him?

The instruction that we have been given, to watch therefore, could be either a positive or a negative watching, could it not?

Let's turn to Matthew 24:42-51. Jesus was talking to His disciples. They were on top of the Mount of Olives. The disciples had been questioning Jesus about the signs of His coming and of the end of the world. They were still expecting Him to set up His kingdom in the near future, and they wanted to know what to watch for so they would be ready when it happened.

"Watch, therefore: for ye know not what hour your Lord doth come. But know this, that if the goodman of the house had known in what watch the thief would come, he would have watched, and would not have suffered his house to be broken up. Therefore be ye also ready: for in such an hour as ye think not the Son of man cometh. Who then is a faithful and wise servant, whom his lord hath made ruler over his household, to give them meat in due season? Blessed is that servant, whom his lord when he cometh shall find so doing. Verily I say unto you, That he shall make him ruler over all his goods. But and if that evil servant shall say in his heart, My lord delayeth his coming [Notice who it is that says, "My lord delayeth his coming." It is the evil servant!] And shall begin to smite his fellowservants, and to eat and drink with the drunken; the lord of that servant shall come in a day when he looketh not for him, and in an hour that he is not aware of. And shall cut him asunder, and appoint him his portion with the hypocrites: there shall be weeping and gnashing of teeth."

The challenge here in Matthew 24 is to stay ready, instead of using what looks like a delay to go out and get drunk—and there are other ways of going out and getting drunk than going out and getting drunk. Getting drunk would represent whatever you do that dulls your spiritual senses and puts the things of God and eternity on the back burner. Jesus gives a strong warning for the one who says, My Lord delayeth his coming; therefore I will forget about Him for awhile and do as I please.

There's something else in this chapter, Matthew 24, that we should notice here. Back in verse 36, it says, speaking of the return of Christ, "Of that day and hour knoweth no man, no, not the angels of heaven, but my Father only." God the Father knows the time of Christ's coming, which means that there must be some point that is settled and established concerning when Jesus comes again.

This would also mean that if we talk about a delay in His coming or the hastening of His coming that these are only in appearance, for the time of His coming is known to the Father.

If I say that I'm going to be home for supper at six o'clock, but I tarry and do not arrive home until eight o'clock, then there is a point past which I tarried, right? Or, if I say I'm going to get home at six o'clock, but I hasten my homecoming, and arrive at five o'clock, then there was a point before which I hastened my coming. If there was no set time for supper or for my return home, then it could not be said that I hastened or delayed coming home for supper. Whatever happens in terms of the hastening or the delay in the coming of Jesus would be the same thing, for a time has been set which the Father knows. The angels don't know when it is, and neither do we. But the Father does.

We often speak about hastening the coming of Jesus, and we often have mottos about working to hasten His coming. Have you ever seen one of those camp meeting banners which read, "Let us arise and finish the work"? Have you ever heard someone urge a congregation to help finish the work so that Christ can return? Look at Romans 9:28, where it says, "He will finish the work, and cut it short in righteousness." So any hastening of the time of the second advent, any cutting short of the time, is God's work, because it's His job to finish whatever needs to be finished. Even though God knows the time of the second advent, even the day and hour, it says He will cut it short.

We might speculate whether the time is cut short in terms of our expectations or cut short in terms of world survival or perhaps some other factor besides simple time. But whatever it means, God still knows when it's going to happen.

What I'd like to suggest is that the point of the return of

Jesus that has been set is not based upon the clock. We're used to being slaves to the clock. And it's going to be a real privilege someday to discover that we will no longer have to worry about time. But God has never been restricted to time, and so, could it be possible that when Inspiration speaks of a hastening or delay in the coming of Christ, that it is speaking about conditions?

With that in mind, let's take a look at the Old Testament record of the children of Israel, just prior to their entrance into the land of Canaan. Did you know that the modern advent people are repeating the history of the Exodus people? You can read about it in volume 5 of the *Testimonies to the Church,* page 160. "Satan's snares are laid for us as verily as they were laid for the children of Israel just prior to their entrance into the land of Canaan. We are repeating the history of that people."

One of the most exciting studies in which I have gotten involved is the study of the comparison between the Exodus and Advent movements. Elder Taylor Bunch did the original work on that, years ago, and opened up a whole library of interesting insights. You can read the book that came as a result of my own study in that area entitled *From Exodus to Advent.* But there are some questions answered in that study that can only be answered by that study. And if we are repeating the history of Israel, then the history of that people should have special interest and meaning for us today.

But let's notice briefly one of the major points regarding the timing of the entrance into the Promised Land. "It was not the will of God that Israel should wander forty years in the wilderness; He desired to lead them directly to the land of Canaan and establish them there, a holy, happy people. But 'they could not enter in because of unbelief.' Hebrews 3:19. Because of their backsliding and apostasy they perished in the desert, and others were raised up to enter the Promised Land. In like manner, it was not the will of God that the coming of Christ should be so long delayed and His people should remain so many years in this world of sin and sorrow. But unbelief separated them from God. As they refused to do the work which He had appointed them, others were raised up to proclaim the message. In mercy to the world, Jesus delays His coming, that sinners may have an opportunity to hear the warning and find in Him a shelter before the wrath of God shall be poured out."—*The Great Controversy*, p. 458.

Now let's take a look at the reason why the children of Israel finally entered the Promised Land. God had intended that they enter into Canaan sooner than they did. But what was it that finally brought an end to their wandering in the wilderness?

Let's go first to Deuteronomy 9:4-7. You recall that the people of Israel had crossed the desert and were finally on the borders of the Promised Land for the second time. Just before Moses died, he repeated to them the history of God's dealings with them. It was Moses' last speech to the people before he took his lonely journey up Mount Nebo.

And he says, verse 4, "Speak not thou in thine heart, after that the Lord thy God hath cast them out from before thee, saying, For my righteousness the Lord hath brought me in to possess this land." So whatever the reason they were entering the Land of Promise, it was not because of their righteousness. Notice the reason: "But for the wickedness of these nations the Lord doth drive them out from before thee. Not for thy righteousness, or for the uprightness of thine heart, dost thou go to possess their land: but for the wickedness of these nations the Lord thy God doth drive them out from before thee, and that he may perform the word which the Lord sware unto thy fathers, Abraham, Isaac, and Jacob." Verse 5.

He continues, "Understand therefore, that the Lord thy God giveth thee not this good land to possess it for thy righteousness; for thou art a stiffnecked people. Remember, and forget not, how thou provokedst the Lord thy God to wrath in the wilderness: from the day that thou didst depart out of the land of Egypt, until ye came unto this place, ye have been rebellious against the Lord." Verses 6, 7. This was one point Moses really nailed down!

Now let's go to the very end of the book, chapter 31:27. Moses is just about finished with his sermon, and he says, "I know thy rebellion, and thy stiff neck: behold, while I am yet alive with you this day, ye have been rebellious against the Lord; and how much more after my death?" He didn't hold out much hope for a change, did he? And he reminds them repeatedly that when they finally enter the Promised Land, it will not be because of their great righteousness, but because of the great wickedness of the Canaanite peoples.

We are repeating the history of that people. We can read from *Christ's Object Lessons,* page 69, "Christ is waiting with longing desire for the manifestation of Himself in His church. When the character of Christ shall be perfectly reproduced in His people, then He will come to claim them as His own." And we have gotten the impression that Christ will wait, endlessly, for His character to be reproduced in us, so that we will become righteous enough to enter the heavenly Canaan.

Now in saying this, I am *not* saying that God's people are going to continue in rebellion right up to the day of the second advent of Christ. But we may be too optimistic if we think that every member of the church is going to stay in the church and have the character of Christ perfectly reproduced in him.

It didn't happen with the people of Israel. Some interesting things took place right on the borders of the Promised Land. The people who were rebellious were shaken out, and the people who entered the Promised Land were people of faith, a remnant of the millions who left Egypt. But they finally entered the Promised Land at a certain point in time because the nations of Canaan had filled up their cup of iniquity, and God could no longer wait, even to give further opportunity to those who were still in rebellion against Him.

With that in mind, let's go to Revelation 11:18, where we find the ultimate reason why Jesus finally comes back to this earth. "The nations were angry, and thy wrath is come, and the time of the dead, that they should be judged, and that thou shouldest give reward unto thy servants the prophets, and to the saints, and them that fear thy name, small and great; and shouldest destroy them which destroy the earth."

Another translation says, "destroy them that corrupt the earth." So there will come a time at the end of the world, a certain point, when the world has filled up its cup of iniquity and corruption. And that time will come, regardless of what you or I do, or don't do, regardless of what you or I am—or we aren't.

Put with this verse in Revelation a comment found in *Testimonies*, volume 5, page 208. "With unerring accuracy the Infinite One still keeps an account with all nations. While His mercy is tendered, with calls to repentance, this account will remain open; but when the figures reach a certain amount which God has fixed, the ministry of His wrath commences. The account is closed. Divine patience ceases. There is no more pleading of mercy in their behalf."

Well, we were told that we could have hastened the coming of the Lord, but we didn't—true or false? True. We were told before the turn of the century that we could have had the privilege of hastening His return. But we didn't, and God knew that we wouldn't; therefore God still knew the day and the hour. And some of us feel that we have already gone through all of the sands in the hourglass and used up the time during which we might have hastened His coming. We are fast approaching the time when He will say, "Here I come, ready or not."

Oh, someone says, "But the gospel has to go to all the world first! And if we look at it with human understanding, there's not a ghost of a chance. People are still being born faster than we are taking the gospel. In fact, when you put all of the Christian denominations together, let alone those that preach the third angel's message, people are still being born faster than the gospel is being spread. We know that, if we face the statistics, we don't have a ghost of a chance of finishing God's work."

But we were told a long time ago that the angels are going to move in and do what we might have had the privilege of doing. The props are set up; God's methods are available. All He needs is a few Shadrachs, Meshachs, and Abednegos, and the whole world can be warned overnight.

So let's not sit around waiting for every member of the world church to perfectly reflect the image of Jesus. And let's not relax, thinking that at our present rate of growth, it will be a long time before the gospel goes to all the world. I believe that those who are shaken in, instead of shaken out, of God's church at the end of time, will perfectly reflect the image of Jesus. And I believe that the gospel is going to go to the whole world. But I also believe that the coming of Jesus is not going to be delayed, for His purposes know no haste and no delay.

God's purposes are moving forward steadily toward fulfillment. The choice is with us, whether we will work with Him, or against Him. But regardless of our choice, His purposes will be accomplished. What a challenge to enter into the relationship with Him and to accept His grace today, so that instead of panic, the nearness of His coming causes us to lift up our heads and rejoice, because our redemption draws near.

Chapter 4
The Loud Cry of the Third Angel

"And after these things I saw another angel come down from heaven, having great power; and the earth was lightened with his glory."

This is what has been called the fourth angel's message. In our subculture it is known as the loud cry of the third angel, although the content of the fourth angel's message most closely resembles the message of the second angel! But it continues, in Revelation 18:2-4: "He cried mightily with a strong voice, saying, Babylon the great is fallen, is fallen, and is become the habitation of devils, and the hold of every foul spirit, and a cage of every unclean and hateful bird. For all nations have drunk of the wine of the wrath of her fornication, and the kings of the earth have committed fornication with her, and the merchants of the earth are waxed rich through the abundance of her delicacies. And I heard another voice from heaven, saying, Come out of her, my people, that ye be not partakers of her sins, and that ye receive not of her plagues."

Now once in a while we hear that the loud cry must have started because there have been a lot of baptisms down in South American somewhere, or the loud cry has begun because somebody doubled his Ingathering goal. But if you've studied the loud cry and the latter rain, you know that when it is given, nobody who receives it will have any question about what's happening. It will be a time when the message of God goes like fire among the stubble—everywhere. The sick are going to be healed, perhaps even the dead will be raised. There is going to be a fantastic manifestation of the power of God that will happen in such a way to make even the Day of Pentecost and the early apostolic church look small by comparison. So in considering the drama of the last-day events, this is a vital message to study.

You may notice as we proceed that we are not necessarily trying to study the last-day events in their exact sequence. For one thing, there is a lot of overlapping and paralleling in the final hours of earth's history. And even though we will surrender to the temptation to include a brief chart at the end of this book, its purpose is not to provide a detailed chronology of the closing scenes.

The loud cry message comes after the shaking time (see *Early Writings,* pages 269-273) and continues until the end of probation. But let's consider first of all what the loud cry message is all about.

There's a one-liner from the pen of Ellen White, found in the *Review and Herald* of April 1, 1890: "Justification by faith . . . is the third angel's message in verity." What does *verity* mean? It means "in truth, in reality." That's what it's all about. The term *justification by faith* is also used interchangeably with *righteousness by faith.* So the third angel's message is a message about righteousness by faith.

Now let's go to another one-liner. It's from an Ellen White article in the *Review and Herald,* September 3, 1889: "There is not one in one hundred who understands for himself the Bible truth on this subject [justification by faith]."

In algebra or geometry, (I don't remember which one!) we learned that two things that are equal to the same thing are equal to each other. So if justification by faith is the third angel's message, and not one in one hundred understood for himself the message of justification by faith, then not one in one hundred understood the third angel's message. Is that safe to say? And can we claim that things are any different now than they were back when the statement was made?

In the previous chapter we noticed that the people of God, just before the return of Christ, have been compared to the people of Israel just before their entrance into the Promised Land. Now let's find a second comparison. *Selected Messages,* book 1, page 406: "The trials of the children of Israel, and their attitude just before the first coming of Christ, have been presented before me again and again to illustrate the position of the people of God in their experience before the second coming of Christ—how the enemy sought every occasion to take control of the minds of the Jews, and today he is seeking to blind the minds of God's servants, that they may not be able to discern the precious truth." So we have been compared to two groups—the people of God in their journey from Egypt to Canaan, and the people of God just prior to the first advent of Christ.

These comparisons are not necessarily complimentary! But there is one comforting truth: in spite of their failures and mistakes and misunderstandings, they were still the people of God, and you can be one of God's people as well.

There's a first cousin to that last quotation. It is found in *Testimonies,* volume 5, page 456: "The same disobedience and failure which were seen in the Jewish church have characterized in a greater degree the people who have had this great light from heaven in the last messages of warning." If you want to find out what the people of God were like at the time of Christ's first advent, just look in the mirror.

Add to that one more line, from the book *The Great Controversy,* page 568, for an even more startling comparison: "There is a striking similarity between the Church of Rome and the Jewish Church at the time of Christ's first advent." Now before you throw this book in the fire, may I remind you that these are not my words! I'm glad they are not my words! But we need to underscore once again that we can still be God's people. But if the people of God before Christ's advent and those before His second advent and the Church of Rome all have something in common, we would do well to take heed to the warning that's being given, wouldn't we?

It would be a grave mistake to assume that because we have some prophetic and historical understanding about the three angels' messages that we are secure from the delusions of the last days. We not only need to understand the message of the three angels, which will swell to loud cry proportions and belt the earth in the time just ahead. We also need to have the personal experience in the spiritual truths that the three angels' messages and the loud cry message is all about. What is that message? I'd like to propose that it goes much deeper than merely a warning about the judgment and Babylon and the beast. It involves more than getting everyone to attend church on Saturday. And in seeking to understand what is involved, we are going to look at a few more comments from the same author who made the comparisons with our church in the first place. And I trust you still have confidence in this messenger to the remnant church.

Let's notice first of all the beginning of the loud cry message. *Review and Herald,* November 22, 1892: "The time of test is just upon us, for the loud cry of the third angel has already begun in the revelation of the righteousness of Christ, the sin-pardoning Redeemer. This is the beginning of the light of the angel whose glory shall fill the whole earth." So what is the beginning of the loud cry? It is the message of the righteousness of Christ.

Now the beginning of the loud cry message, around 1888 in our history, faded and was largely lost sight of for many years. But it is not lost, and when it begins again, it will be carried forward to its final fulfillment. But when the time comes for it to again rise to the top, *it will begin with the message of Christ our righteousness.*

Now turn to *Testimonies to Ministers,* page 92: "All power

is given into His [Jesus'] hands, that He may dispense rich gifts unto men, imparting the priceless gift of His own righteousness to the helpless human agent. This is the message that God commanded to be given to the world. It is the third angel's message, which is to be proclaimed with a loud voice, and attended with the outpouring of His Spirit in a large measure." So what is the content of the loud cry message? It's a message about the righteousness of Christ, imparted to the helpless human agent. So the message of the righteousness of Christ is not only the beginning, it is the content of the loud cry of the third angel. It is the heart of that message.

And finally, go to *Testimonies,* volume 6, page 19: "The message of Christ's righteousness is to sound from one end of the earth to the other to prepare the way of the Lord. This is the glory of God, which closes the work of the third angel." So the message of Christ and His righteousness is the beginning, the content, and the end of the loud cry of the third angel. Do you have any question about that?

If this is true, then no wonder the devil hates it. You are probably aware that in the last few years the devil has really taken a swing at the message of righteousness by faith. He has tried to bring it into such ill repute that we would forget about it and go on to "more important" things. Have you picked that up? The church became involved in controversy concerning the sanctuary and judgment and some of the prophecies of Daniel and Revelation, and now many are afraid to talk much about righteousness by faith, afraid they will rock the boat again.

At a workers' meeting in the South not long ago, one young preacher stood up and said, "Why is it that some of you keep talking about the same thing all the time—righteousness by faith? Why don't you go on to something else? Why don't you talk about something more important, like church growth?"

Now I don't know if he said this with tongue-in-cheek or

not. I hope he did. But we were told a long time ago that the devil is not willing that this message of Christ's righteousness be clearly revealed or understood, because he knows that if we receive it fully, his power will be broken. And if that is the case, then we have a heavy responsibility never to lose sight of this message.

So if we are interested in taking the message of the three angels to the world, and if we understand that message correctly, we will have the message of righteousness by faith as the main thrust of those three messages.

So when we read the first angel's message, "Fear God, and give glory to him; for the hour of his judgment is come: and worship him," we look at it in the light of the message of righteousness by faith. What does it mean to fear God? It doesn't mean to be afraid of Him, but to hold Him in awe. What does it mean to give glory to God? This immediately triggers the classic definition of justification by faith, found in *Testimonies to Ministers,* page 456: "What is justification by faith? It is the work of God in laying the glory of man in the dust, and doing for man that which it is not in his power to do for himself."

What is it that we can't do for ourselves? We can't save ourselves. We can't save ourselves from our past sins, we can't save ourselves from our present sinning, and we can't save ourselves from the world of sin. We are stuck! We have all made the mistake of getting born on the wrong planet! We are in trouble, and our only hope is in a Saviour. It is the systems of false religion that are based on the idea that we can save ourselves. And our greatest danger today is to think that we can in some way save ourselves.

"And worship Him." What does it mean to worship Him? Well, it means that we worship God instead of ourselves. If we think there is some way in which we can save ourselves, then we take part of the glory for ourselves, and we end up worshiping ourselves instead of worshiping God. And it's the warning against this danger that is given in the time of the three angels and swells to a loud cry with the message of the fourth angel.

You may say, "Oh, I know I can't save myself. That warning must be for someone else." But in spite of saying the right words, the practice of the majority of church members screams what they really believe. Because when the majority of church members are finding no time, day by day, to spend seeking Jesus and His salvation, they are trying to save themselves, regardless of the words they speak. Because it is only in coming to Jesus each day and spending time in worshiping and glorifying Him and learning to trust in Him, that we are saved from trying to save ourselves.

My brother joined me in a week of prayer at Pacific Union College not long ago, and he preached a powerful sermon one evening on the fact that everybody has a devotional life. He said, Don't talk about those who have a devotional life and those who do not. Everybody has a devotional life.

Some people are devoted to rock music—that's their devotional life. Some people are devoted to the stock market. They spend hours reading the fine print that would bore the rest of us to death. That's their devotional life. Some people are devoted to their own appearance, and that's where their focus is placed. Some are devoted to sports. They don't say, "I know I should spend an hour reading the sports page in the newspaper, but it's hard to find the time. My mind wanders." No, they are so devoted to sports that when they sit down with the sports section of the newspaper, they don't know where the time went.

What an insult is offered to the King of kings by those who claim to be His people when they find it hard to spend time thinking and talking of Him. If we are going to worship Him, we will not be worshiping ourselves. And that's the common thread of all of the angels' messages in Revelation—the warning against self-worship and the invitation to worship God. Babylon and the beast, which get such bad marks, are condemned because of their organized system of self-worship. But it is possible even as a member of the "remnant church" to fall into the very trap we are warning others against, when we find time for everybody and everything, except for the God we profess to worship.

With that in mind, let's turn our attention to the loud cry message specifically, as we try to understand a little more of its meaning and importance.

As we noticed earlier, the message of the fourth angel of Revelation 18 is similar to the message of the second angel of Revelation 14 and includes a warning against Babylon, which is fallen. But Babylon was fallen to begin with, wasn't it? Remember the tower of Babel, from which Babylon got its beginnings? It was an attempt of mankind to save themselves, and it fell a long time ago. But Babylon in prophecy represents fallen religious systems. Babylon, the great, the mother of harlots, is not antireligious—it is religious to its very core. But Babylon has a problem.

The problem of modern Babylon, and ancient Babylon as well, is represented by the term *fornication*. Fornication is the merging of two bodies that aren't supposed to merge. And within the religious system of Babylon, the two things that merge are the concepts of salvation by faith and salvation by works.

Arthur Spaulding, in his book *Captains of the Host,* makes the observation that most professed Christians believe "that man must strive to be good and to do good, and that when he has done all he can, Christ will come to his aid and help him do the rest. In this confused credo of salvation partly by works and partly with auxiliary power, many trust today."— Page 601.

Have you ever told your children to be good? Have you ever had someone say to you, "Be good," and you answered, "I'll try." For most of us, it sounds familiar, doesn't it? We think that we are supposed to do everything we can in our own power, and God will make up the difference where we fall short.

Particularly in the area of living the Christian life, we find it easy to fall into the pattern of trying to make ourselves do what we know we should be doing and gritting our teeth and trying to force ourselves to be obedient. And it is this subsidy religion, subsidy sanctification, which is Babylon. It's been around for a long time. But it is Babylon nonetheless. And the loud cry message comes when God's people discover that when we seek Jesus and learn to know Him better and come into deeper fellowship with Him, that He is the One who produces all of the righteousness. We don't produce any of it. Therefore, He is the One who receives all of the glory. We don't receive any of it.

The truth is that God's power plus man's power equals no power, and that is the reason for many of our defeats in the Christian life. We have held on to the fornication principle, the principle of Babylon, even while preaching against Babylon in our efforts to warn the world about the crisis to come.

The combination of religious and secular power is a deadly combination. During the Dark Ages, the beast power wasn't just a religious power—and it wasn't just a political power. It was a combination of the two—fornication. Now notice the description in the book *The Great Controversy,* page 445: "When the leading churches in the United States, uniting upon such points of doctrine as are held by them in common, shall influence the state to enforce their decrees and to sustain their institutions, then Protestant America will have formed an image to the Roman hierarchy, and the infliction of civil penalties upon dissenters will inevitably result." Then comes this statement. "But in the very act of enforcing a religious duty by secular power, the churches would themselves form an image to the beast."—Page 449.

All right, what is the image to the beast? It is enforcing a religious duty by secular power. And what's another word for secular power? Human power. Therefore the image to the beast involves trying to enforce religious duty by human power.

We can talk about the image to the beast and the mark of the beast and the number and name of the beast. And we can look at it solely in terms of prophetic and historical events. But there is something far deeper involved. We don't have to join the beast, or Babylon, to become involved in trying to enforce religious duties by secular power. And while it is true that in the end, those who are a part of Babylon and the beast are going to choose a particular day of worship as a symbol of their power, it is possible to be attending church on Saturday every week and still be guilty of trying to use your human power to enforce your religious beliefs. And that's Babylon. That's the image to the beast. That's fornication.

In the end, the Sabbath of the fourth commandment becomes a symbol of the opposite pole. Those who honor the Sabbath have come to understand the blessing of the Sabbath rest, spoken of in the fourth chapter of Hebrews, the rest that remains for the people of God. You can read it in verses 9 and 10. "There remaineth therefore a rest to the people of God. For he that is entered into his rest, he also hath ceased from his own works, as God did from his." Those who rest from their own attempts to force themselves to keep the law of God are those who have accepted of the righteousness of Christ, and His righteousness lived out in their lives, through His power instead of their own. And it is this message that the loud cry message involves. It is this message that is the message of the third angel in verity.

In this context, the national Sunday law that we have heard so much about in our subculture becomes more than just a law about a particular day of the week. It becomes a symbol of the belief held in common by the churches and people who have rejected the Sabbath rest, the rest from our own works. It becomes an attempt to force everyone to submit to the principle of Babylon, to attempt to save ourselves instead of accepting the salvation provided.

But even within the "remnant" church, this understanding comes slowly. Even for the people of God, it is hard to learn, and easy to forget, that in Jesus is our only hope of salvation. We sing it, we pray it, we preach it—*but we often fail to live it.*

Zacharias, the father of John the Baptist, found it hard to remember, even though he was a righteous man, a priest, and chosen by God to train and educate the messenger of the Messiah. You can read it in *The Desire of Ages,* page 98: "The birth of a son to Zacharias, like the birth of the child of Abraham, and that of Mary, was to teach a great spiritual truth, a truth that we are slow to learn and ready to forget. In ourselves we are incapable of doing any good thing; but that which we cannot do will be wrought by the power of God in every submissive and believing soul. It was through faith that the child of promise was given. It is through faith that spiritual life is begotten, and we are enabled to do the works of righteousness."

Notice—it is through faith that two things happen. First, through faith spiritual life is begotten. But it doesn't stop there. It is also through faith, not through our own efforts, that we are enabled to do the works of righteousness.

Not only does the attempt to save ourselves fail of its object, but it actually prevents the working of God for our salvation. "The effort to earn salvation by one's own works inevitably leads men to pile up human exactions as a barrier against sin. For, seeing that they fail to keep the law, they will devise rules and regulations of their own to force themselves to obey. All this turns the mind away from God to self."—*Thoughts From the Mount of Blessing,* p. 123.

Here's another description of the same problem: "While [some] think they are committing themselves to God, there is a great deal of self-dependence. There are conscientious souls that trust partly to God, and partly to themselves. They do not look to God, to be kept by His power, but depend upon watchfulness against temptation, and the performance of certain duties for acceptance with Him. There are no victories in this kind of faith. Such persons toil to no purpose; their souls are in continual bondage, and they find no rest until their burdens are laid at the feet of Jesus."— *Selected Messages,* bk. 1, p. 353.

For those who find no rest in their struggle against sin and the devil there is good news. It's found in Matthew 11:28. Jesus Himself gives the invitation. "Come unto me, . . . and I will give you rest." The rest from the problem of Babylon is to be found in coming to Jesus and accepting His grace day by day. That is still all we can do toward our own salvation. Just come. And keep coming to Him. That's the secret.

And in the time of the three angels, God's people finally reach the understanding of where the power is. They go through extreme struggles. You can read about it in the chapter already referred to about the shaking, in *Early Writings,* page 269-273. But after all of the darkness and confusion and perplexity and anxiety, something finally dawns. And when it does, God's people receive the victory and go forth with their faces lighted up, to proclaim the full message of the righteousness of Christ with a loud cry. And the message goes from one end of the earth to the other.

Some of us believe we are living on the verge of that breakthrough. The church has gone through struggles to understand clearly the message of justification by faith and pardon and forgiveness. But the subject of sanctification by faith and how to live the victorious Christian life is still shrouded in mystery in the minds of many. There may be crises involved in coming to a full understanding of the message of Christ's righteousness as lived out in the life. Yet the understanding will come, and the loud cry will begin, and continue, and be completed as the message of Christ our Righteousness is proclaimed with a loud cry throughout all the earth.

Chapter 5
It's Going to Rain!

There's a song that most of us probably remember that talks about the rain that's coming.

Showers of blessing,
Showers of blessing we need,
Mercy drops round us are falling,
But for the showers we plead.

The outpouring of the Holy Spirit has often been compared to rain, and the rain we want to consider in this context has been called the "latter rain." What does that mean? Well, it means the Spirit of God being poured out for the last time, the final time, before the coming of Christ.

The Holy Spirit has been around for a long time! He shows up in Genesis 1:2, involved in the work of creation. He was present in Old Testament times, moving in the hearts of men to convict, to convert, to cleanse, and then to commission them for service. You can read about His work in turning Saul, the newly anointed king of Israel, into "another man." See 1 Samuel 10. He descended in the form of a dove at the time of Jesus' baptism. And He came in a special sense at Pentecost. It would take a long time to list all of the examples given in Scripture of the working of the Spirit of God. But we have been promised that the Holy Spirit will come with particular power at the very end, just before the close of probation, to do His final work in the earth.

So when we talk about the latter rain, we are talking about another outpouring of the Spirit of God such as has been experienced by God's people in the ages, only this time it's in greater power and scope—and it's the last to come before the end of time.

We have noticed the content of the loud cry message, the message upon which the Holy Spirit is going to be given, so that the loud cry can go from one end of the earth to the other in a short period of time. We have seen that the loud cry is about the righteousness of Jesus and His power to save and that it results in the glory of man being humbled in the dust. Now let's turn our study to the distinguishing marks of the latter rain of the Holy Spirit, as it is poured out upon the earth to enable the loud cry message to do its work.

In the first place, God is going to take the reins into His own hands, and we are going to be surprised at the simple means that He will use to bring about and perfect His work in righteousness. You can read about that in *Testimonies to Ministers,* page 300.

What does God taking the reins into His own hands mean to you?

I used to go to town with my Aunt Lucy. Aunt Lucy had an old gray mare named Nell, and when we visited Grandma's house, we'd ride into town in the back of the carriage with Aunt Lucy and old Nell. I was three years old, and I wasn't about to take the reins into my own hands! I was happy to leave the driving to Aunt Lucy! Perhaps a more modern analogy would be to say that God is going to take the wheel. The prediction is that He will take control of events and bring about the finishing of His own work. I'm looking forward to that happening, aren't you?

There's another insight given in *The Great Controversy,* page 612. In the context of the latter rain, Ellen White writes that, "The message will be carried not so much by argument as by the deep conviction of the Spirit of God. The arguments have been presented. The seed has been sown, and now it will spring up and bear fruit. . . . Truth is seen in its clearness, and the honest children of God sever the bands which have held them. Family connections, church relations, are powerless to stay them now." Nothing can now keep them from obedience to the truth.

No longer will the excuse be given, I can't accept the truth because my husband or wife or parents or children aren't willing to accept it. When the Holy Spirit comes with power, all human considerations will be set aside, and hearts everywhere will respond to His invitation.

Another interesting insight, from the book *Early Writings,* page 277, is that as the angels come to aid the mighty angel of Revelation 18, the message will seem to come as an addition to the message of the three angels. We already noticed in the previous chapter that the message of the loud cry is similar in many ways to the message of the second angel. But the loud cry message, about the righteousness of Christ, will seem to be in addition to that. The message of salvation by faith alone in Jesus Christ began back in 1888 as the understanding of the three angels' messages began to be more clearly understood. But the message of the fourth angel will be distinct and will seem to be brand new, in a sense, even though it is part and parcel of the message already given, the very heart of the three angels' messages.

Here's another insight that is significant. Under the showers of the latter rain, as at the time of Pentecost, people will hear the truth spoken in their own tongue. The events of the Day of Pentecost, will be repeated. "Thousands of voices will be imbued with the power to speak forth the wonderful truths of God's Word. The stammering tongue will be unloosed, and the timid will be made strong to bear courageous testimony to the truth."—*Review and Herald,* July 20, 1886.

If you are timid, welcome to the club! Some of us are so bashful that it hurts. I used to complain to my father about it, and he said, "Don't worry, son, we're all bashful when we're young. You'll get over it." But instead, it gets worse every year! But I can testify to the fact that when you get up and try to say something for Jesus that He takes over and gives you courage beyond your natural personality. It's good news, isn't it? Even the most timid and retiring may be given a place as one of the voices for God to swell the loud cry at the time of the latter rain, as the message of Christ and His righteousness goes like fire among the stubble.

Here's another prediction for the time of the latter rain. The supernatural manifestations of the power of God will be revived. "Miracles will be wrought, the sick will be healed, and signs and wonders will follow the believers."— *The Great Controversy*, p. 612. It will be an exciting time to be alive!

But there is an interesting comment in *Testimonies*, volume 5, page 80, regarding the work that is to be accomplished. "In the last solemn work few great men will be engaged. They are self-sufficient, independent of God, and He cannot use them." And another first cousin to that, found in *Counsels on Health*, page 367: "It is a dangerous age for any man who has talents which can be of value in the work of God; for Satan is constantly plying his temptations upon such a person, ever trying to fill him with pride and ambition; and when God would use him, in nine cases out of ten he becomes independent, self-sufficient, and feels capable of standing alone."

How often "God hath chosen the weak things of the world to confound the things which are mighty." 1 Corinthians 1:27. How often those of the greatest natural talents and abilities and gifts have turned to their own ways, while those who seem to be the least qualified for the work are used by God in the greatest capacity.

Have you ever looked back through one of your school annuals and pondered how many of the apparent "great" people on campus during school days ended up being lost sight of in later years, while some of the least promising ones went on to important positions in the service of God? It's a pattern that's hard to miss if you have your eyes open.

Do you consider yourself to be a great person? Watch out! Are you afraid God can never use you for anything important, because you have little to commend you as a worker for Him? There's good news! If you give yourself to Him, He can use you to do a great work for Him.

Here's something else to expect during the time of the latter rain. "Under the showers of the latter rain the inventions of man, the human machinery, will at times be swept away, the boundary of man's authority will be as broken reeds, and the Holy Spirit will speak through the living, human agent, with convincing power. No one then will watch to see if the sentences are well rounded off, if the grammar is faultless. The living water will flow in God's own channels."—*Selected Messages*, bk. 2, p. 58, 59.

On the day of Pentecost, when the Holy Spirit was poured out upon the early Christian church, thousands were converted in a day. God's blessing was manifest in a remarkable way. And yet, there were some who were unable to appreciate what was taking place. You can read about their response in Acts 2:13. They concluded that Peter and the other apostles were drunk. So it will be in the time of the latter rain. The Holy Spirit is going to be falling on hearts all around, while many will not even recognize it or appreciate it. See *Review and Herald*, March 2, 1897.

We have been told that angels are going to show up to do the work that we were given the privilege of doing, but neglected to do. We are going to hear someone speaking, proclaiming God's message with power, and we'll say, "Where is he from? Who is he?"

And the only answer will be, "I don't know." There will be those whose origin we will be unable to trace. Angels have shown up in human form on many occasions in the history of this world. We have evidence of it in Scripture. And it still happens on occasion, even today. Some years ago a pastor in Phoenix, Arizona, requested Elder Johns, the religious liberty secretary for the Pacific Union, to come to his assistance. The pastor was nervous because there was a big meeting being held by civic and political leaders in Phoenix, where they were going to discuss the Sunday blue laws. So the Sunday proponents had a dinner, and chose a well-known lawyer renowned for his glibness, to present their case for blue laws in Arizona.

The local Adventist pastor notified the union conference, and Elder Johns came to attend the dinner along with him. Elder Johns said that when the lawyer showed up, he was so eloquent and presented his case with such apparent logic, that the group was convinced to follow his suggestions and proceed with definite moves in the direction of enforcing the Sunday blue laws.

The local pastor thought he should say something to try to counteract the lawyer's presentation, but when he stood up to speak, he found himself unable to say a word. He said that his whole mouth felt like it was full of cotton. After trying for a few moments, he gave up and sat down.

Elder Johns then decided it was up to him to save the day, so he stood up. When they compared notes later, they found that they both experienced the same inability to speak. Elder Johns' mouth also went dry, and he was not able to say a word.

As they slumped in their seats, wondering what was going on, the door opened and in walked a man in a pin-striped business suit. He approached the microphone and said, "I am a citizen, and I would like to say something." And in a few paragraphs he made the lawyer's arguments look like nothing. The place became deathly still. The lawyer attempted to refute his arguments but was obviously confused, and the meeting ended in confusion.

Elder Johns and the local pastor tried to find the man in the business suit at the close of the meeting, but he was gone! You would expect that, wouldn't you? He was gone. Elder Johns told me that in all of his forty years of ministry, he had never had a more inspiring moment than that one. I don't blame him, do you?

We can expect supernatural help in the times ahead, and all along the way God has kindly given us samples of what is available!

But notice this solemn warning. "The light which will lighten the earth with its glory will be called a false light, by those who refuse to walk in its advancing glory."—*Review and Herald,* May 27, 1890. And one more reference, and then we're done. "There is to be in the churches a wonderful manifestation of the power of God, but it will not move upon those who have not humbled themselves before the Lord, and opened the door of their heart by confession and repentance. In the manifestation of that power which lightens the earth with the glory of God, they will see only something which in their blindness they think dangerous, something which will arouse their fears, and they will brace themselves to resist it."—*Maranatha,* p. 219.

The devil is trying to do everything possible to bring the message of Christ our Righteousness into ill repute, so that people will think it dangerous and brace their feet to resist it. We have already seen enough evidence of the way he has worked against this message, haven't we?

But if the loud cry is the message upon which the Holy Spirit is poured out with latter rain power, and if the loud cry message is the message that Christ is our only hope of salvation, then we ought to do everything we can to remain open to that message and to understand that message correctly.

And once again, not only is correct understanding essential, but also a corresponding experience in the faith we profess. If we find no time day by day to accept and experience the saving power of Jesus Christ, then we will not be prepared when the time comes for the final outpouring of His spirit. How can we be ready to receive the latter rain? We will attempt to answer that in more detail in the following chapter.

Chapter 6
Preparation for the Latter Rain

At first glance it might appear that the preparation for the latter rain and the preparation for the coming of Christ are one and the same. But the latter rain itself is a part of the preparation for the coming of Christ. It is part of God's work in getting a people ready to meet Him. You can read about this in *Testimonies*, volume 1, page 187. "Those who come up to every point, and stand every test, and overcome, be the price what it may, have heeded the counsel of the True Witness, and they will receive the latter rain, and *thus be fitted for translation*." (Emphasis supplied.)

So the latter rain is one of God's methods for fitting His people for translation. And in order to receive the latter rain, there must have been some preparation needed.

With that in mind, let's go back to a quick look at the works of the Holy Spirit. We have already listed these briefly, but let's spend a few moments with them once again in this context.

The first work of the Holy Spirit is to convince the world of sin. You can read about His work of conviction in John 16. The second work of the Holy Spirit is in conversion, and that is found in John 3. No one can even see the kingdom of God unless he is born again.

The third work of the Holy Spirit involves a cleansing of the Christian. Romans 8 would be the reference on that. While many of those in the church have responded to the second work of the Spirit and have been converted, not so many have allowed the Spirit to complete His third work in cleansing their lives. Only with those who have seen the importance of the continuing relationship with Christ can the Spirit do His work of changing us into His image.

It is under the third work of the Holy Spirit, His cleansing work, that the fruits of the Spirit are developed: love, joy, peace, long-suffering, and so forth. Also under the third work of the Holy Spirit is what we would call the filling of the Spirit. It is a gradual process, such as filling a cup or vessel. It doesn't happen instantaneously. It involves growth.

The fourth work of the Holy Spirit is to commission for service. And once again, there is a process involved. A baby Christian needs to begin at once to share as much as he knows of the grace of God. Sharing is necessary to growth. But as the Christian matures and the cleansing process continues, the time will come for a fuller manifestation of the Spirit in the life, often referred to as the baptism of the Holy Spirit.

In connection with the study of the latter rain, the fullest manifestation of the baptism of the Holy Spirit will occur during the final outpouring of the Spirit in latter rain power.

One of the reasons it is important to keep these different functions of the Holy Spirit's work in mind is so that we will not lose sight of one very important fact. The baptism of the Holy Spirit, under His fourth work, is always for service. It is never for cleansing. There is no Bible example of the baptism of the Spirit being given for any purpose other than service. It is never to make you holy or to make you happy. It is given to make you useful.

The time of the early rain is the time for the growth and cleansing to take place, so that the Christian will be prepared to receive the latter rain in its fullness. The cleansing work of the Spirit is the time for overcoming and victory and cleansing from sin.

With this in mind, we would consider an oft-asked question in regard to the latter rain. Does the latter rain change our characters? The answer is No. The latter rain does not change our character or our direction. That is the purpose of the early rain.

Let's notice one quotation on that, among the several that we could list. It's found in *Testimonies to Ministers,* page 507: "Many have in a great measure failed to receive the former rain. They have not obtained all the benefits that God has thus provided for them. They expect that the lack will be supplied by the latter rain. When the richest abundance of grace shall be bestowed, they intend to open their hearts to receive it. They are making a terrible mistake. . . . Only those who are living up to the light they have will receive greater light."

So there is something necessary in order to receive the latter rain. It is to have received the early rain. And those who receive the early rain will receive power to overcome and victory over sin.

There are people who have gathered together long compilations of quotations concerning this question. We will list just two or three examples here, to nail down the point, for it is true that overcoming and victory are necessary prerequisites for receiving the latter rain.

"I was shown that if God's people make no efforts on their part, but wait for the refreshing to come upon them and remove their wrongs and correct their errors; if they depend upon that to cleanse them from filthiness of the flesh and spirit, and fit them to engage in the loud cry of the third angel, they will be found wanting."—*Testimonies,* vol. 1, p. 619.

"I saw that many were neglecting the preparation so needful and were looking to the time of 'refreshing' and the 'latter rain' to fit them to stand in the day of the Lord and to live in His sight. Oh, how many I saw in the time of trouble without a shelter! They had neglected the needful preparation; therefore they could not receive the refreshing that all must have to fit them to live in the sight of a holy God."—*Early Writings*, p. 71.

And one more quotation. This one is found in the *Review and Herald* of November 19, 1908. "Only those who have withstood temptation in the strength of the Mighty One will be permitted to act a part in proclaiming it [the third angel's message] when it shall have swelled into the loud cry."

What is your response when you read these kinds of statements? It probably depends upon whether you are looking at them through behavioral glasses or relationship glasses! The behaviorist reads them and says, "Oh, yes. I must begin anew to try to be obedient, to try to overcome, to work hard on being righteous." The relationist says, "The only hope that I have to be prepared for the times ahead is to know and trust Jesus even more. What a challenge and an invitation to continue coming to Him to receive the gift of His righteousness."

For too long we have looked at these kinds of statements and begun to think: "I must." And what we should accept instead is: "He will." There's a big difference between those two, isn't there?

So although victory and overcoming and obedience precede the latter rain, that does not mean that victory and overcoming and obedience are our work, any more than the latter rain is our work. Our work has always been, and always will be, coming to Christ day by day for ourselves. And as we continue to come and to accept the gifts He has to offer, under the early rain experience, He will bring us to the condition of readiness to receive the gift of the latter rain. The bottom line is always the continuing relationship with God, when it comes to our part. But He has made Himself responsible for all the rest of it, so long as we continue to seek Him and to depend upon His strength and righteousness instead of our own.

Let's take a look at several passages of Scripture that are beautiful in describing this experience. The first one is Hebrews 13:20, 21. "The God of peace, that brought again from the dead our Lord Jesus, that great shepherd of the sheep, through the blood of the everlasting covenant, make you perfect in every good work to do his will, working in you that which is wellpleasing in his sight, through Jesus Christ; to whom be glory for ever and ever. Amen." Who is going to do the work? *He* is going to work, *in you*. And how much will that produce? It will produce that which is wellpleasing in His sight, in every good work, doing His will. The work will be complete, but it's His work, it's His department. All we can do is go to Him day by day to receive it.

Now let's go to 2 Corinthians 10:4, 5. "The weapons of our warfare are not carnal, but mighty through God to the pulling down of strong holds; casting down imaginations, and every high thing that exalteth itself against the knowledge of God, and bringing into captivity every thought to the obedience of Christ." Notice the weapons. They are not our weapons—but God's. The battle is won through the forces of heaven, not through our own efforts.

In 2 Chronicles 20 is recorded an Old Testament battle. The enemy was coming. King Jehoshaphat had it straight— for when he heard about the enemy, he went to his knees for a prayer meeting, instead of to the fields for a target practice. They sharpened up their scrolls instead of their spears. And God rewarded them not only with victory, but with a very pointed message before the time of the battle even arrived. He said, first of all, The battle is not yours, but God's. And second, You will not need to fight in this battle.

The stories of the Bible were given for more than simply history lessons. They were given to teach spiritual truth. We can apply the message of 2 Chronicles 20 to ourselves today, when we hear of the enemy coming, as a roaring lion, seeking whom he may devour. We do not need to fight in this battle, for the great controversy is not our battle, but God's. He will bring about His own victory in our behalf.

In conclusion, here is a comment that should bring hope to any heart. "In Christ, God has provided means for subduing every evil trait and resisting every temptation, however strong. But many feel that they lack faith, and therefore they remain away from Christ. Let these souls, in their helpless unworthiness, cast themselves upon the mercy of their compassionate Saviour. Look not to self, but to Christ. He who healed the sick and cast out demons when He walked among men is still the same mighty Redeemer. Then grasp His promises as leaves from the tree of life: 'Him that cometh to Me I will in no wise cast out.' John 6:37. As you come to Him, believe that He accepts you, because He has promised. You can never perish while you do this—never."—*The Ministry of Healing*, pp. 65, 66.

You can never perish while you do what?—while you come to Christ, believing that He accepts you and that He will not cast you out. And as we come to Christ, and continue coming to Him, we find in Him the means for subduing every evil trait and resisting every temptation. It's good news, isn't it? He has the power to finish the work He has begun in our lives and to prepare us for the day of His coming.

Which brings us to one final question: If the work of victory and overcoming must be accomplished *before* the time of the latter rain, but if the latter rain itself prepares us in some way for the coming of Christ, what does the latter rain accomplish? Apparently there are some of the positive graces of the Spirit that are needed in our lives before we are fitted for translation, that go above and beyond merely overcoming sin.

Perhaps a bit of analogy might help. If you expect company, you will probably want to do some preparing of the more negative kind! You may want to scrub the kitchen floor or clean the sink or wash the sheets. There is preparation in removing any defilement from your home and environment. But there is more to getting ready for company than taking out the garbage. You will also want to make some positive preparations. You might want to bake a cake (a carrot cake, or course!), set the table with your best dishes, bring in some fresh flowers from the garden.

So often we think of preparation for Christ's coming in terms of cleaning up the negative aspects of our lives. But in our preparation for the marriage supper of the Lamb, there can be some positive changes that should be made, beyond cleansing of sin, that will make us finally ready for His appearing.

Chapter 7
The 144,000

For a number of years our family lived in the town of Angwin, California, where Pacific Union College is located. PUC is one of the most beautiful Adventist college campuses, located in the mountains of northern California. It was an easy place to decide to move to and a hard place to leave!

But if ever there was an Adventist ghetto, this was it. The church membership from the village was well over 2,000. Add to that another 2,000 college students. In the entire area surrounding the college, there were something like forty families who were not members of the Adventist church, and they had been overcontacted years ago.

Ingathering didn't go too well in Angwin, but when someone in the General Conference came up with the goal of making a visit to every non-Adventist home in the world, Angwin was probably the first to reach its goal!

But there in Angwin, we had several standing jokes. One of them was the observation that PUC was eight miles from the nearest known sin—the distance to the nearest "real" town, complete with a couple of bars and a theater. Once in a while a homemade sign would be taped to the city limits sign at the edge of town, saying, "The Holy City". And, my favorite?—a sign someone put up that read, "Angwin City Limits: population 144,000"!

People have often wondered and speculated and, yes, even

joked about who the 144,000 will be. It's the kind of topic that can keep you going until midnight, or keep your Sabbath School class discussing even after the second bell to dismiss for church! Sometimes 144,000 seems like an awfully small number, particularly as the church membership worldwide continues to increase. Other times, when we read about the qualifications and descriptions of the 144,000, we wonder that God will be able to find so many.

But let's take a position right to begin with (and if you disagree, that's OK!), that the 144,000 will consist of the people who are members of the remnant church, who remain after the shaking is finished. They go out with great power, under the latter rain, to give the loud cry message. And the great multitude, which no man can number, come to join them, to take the place, and perhaps more than make up the number of those who have defected.

There are two primary scriptures in the study of this subject that we should notice. The first, Revelation 14:1-5. "I looked, and, lo, a Lamb stood on the mount Sion, and with him an hundred forty and four thousand, having his Father's name written in their foreheads. And I heard a voice from heaven, as the voice of many waters, and as the voice of a great thunder: and I heard the voice of harpers harping with their harps: and they sung as it were a new song before the throne, and before the four beasts, and the elders: and no man could learn that song but the hundred and forty and four thousand, which were redeemed from the earth. These are they which were not defiled with women; for they are virgins. These are they which follow the Lamb whithersoever he goeth. These were redeemed from among men, being the firstfruits unto God and to the Lamb. And in their mouth was found no guile: for they are without fault before the throne of God."

So the 144,000 are God's people. They have the Father's name written in their foreheads. What do we write our names on? On things that belong to us, right? So these people belong to God. They are redeemed from the earth.

They have not defiled themselves with women. What does a woman represent in Bible prophecy? A church. So they are not defiled with other churches. Theirs is a pure faith. They follow the Lamb whithersoever He goeth, and they are without fault.

Sometimes the Bible uses the term *faultless*, and other times it uses the term *blameless*. Is there a difference? This special group of people are not only blameless, but faultless as well. They have obtained the victory over sin in their lives, and in their mouths is found no guile.

The Greek word rendered "guile" could be translated "fish bait" as the word was used in ancient times. What is fish bait? It's something that appears to be good on the outside, but inside it's not so good. The 144,000 are not only faultless in outward appearance, but their hearts are without fault before God as well. They are the same on the inside as on the outside.

Let's go now to the second passage, which has the rest of the story on the 144,000. It's found in Revelation 7. "After these things I saw four angels standing on the four corners of the earth, holding the four winds of the earth, that the wind should not blow on the earth, nor on the sea, nor on any tree. And I saw another angel ascending from the east, having the seal of the living God: and he cried with a loud voice to the four angels, to whom it was given to hurt the earth and the sea, saying, Hurt not the earth, neither the sea, nor the trees, till we have sealed the servants of our God in their foreheads. And I heard the number of them which were sealed: and there were sealed an hundred and forty and four thousand of all the tribes of the children of Israel." Verses 1-4.

Then the tribes of Israel are listed.

Before we continue, let's back up and notice a few significant points. This group are sealed in their foreheads. What does the forehead represent? It represents the mind, or the thinking capacity. And those who were sealed were from the tribes of the children of Israel. Does that mean just literal Israel? No, because Paul said in Galatians 3:29, "If ye be Christ's, then are ye Abraham's seed, and heirs according to the promise."

In the *Review and Herald*, March 9, 1905, we read: "Let us strive with all the power that God has given us to be among the hundred and forty-four thousand." If that sentence is true, then it should be possible for every one of us to join the 144,000, regardless of our ethnic or national origin, right?

So the promises about the 144,000 are given to spiritual not literal Israel. And you know, if you have grappled with this subject before, the question is not so much who the 144,000 are, but who the great multitude is. But let's continue reading Revelation 7.

"After this I beheld, and, lo, a great multitude, which no man could number, of all nations, and kindreds, and people, and tongues, stood before the throne, and before the Lamb, clothed with white robes, and palms in their hands; and cried with a loud voice, saying, Salvation to our God which sitteth upon the throne, and unto the Lamb." Verses 9, 10.

Do you remember what a palm represents in Bible symbolism? It is a token of victory. Palms were used in the victorious march into Jerusalem at the time of the triumphal entry, just a few days before Jesus was crucified. What does the white robe represent? The righteousness of Christ.

Again we should remember the chapter called "The Shaking," found in *Early Writings* pages 269-273. It describes the great shakedown of God's people, and then it tells of the time when they have obtained the victory and go forth to proclaim the message with a loud voice.

And, by the way, if the mention made so far has not motivated you to go to your bookshelf and get out your copy of *Early Writings* and read the entire chapter on the shaking for yourself, you have missed the point! We will refer to that chapter again. It is a powerful description, compact and concise, describing the events that we are even now beginning to see all around us. It is well worth your time to read and reread.

But notice the sequence. First the 144,000 are given the seal of God. They have obtained the victory, for in the previous passage we were told that they were without fault, and no guile was found in them. Putting this sequence together with the description of the shaking that is given in *Early Writings*, it is clear that after the victory and breakthrough for those who were shaken in instead of shaken out, there comes the time of the loud cry and the latter rain, and great numbers come to take their places with the people of God.

Now notice that the great multitude also are crying with a loud voice, "Salvation to our God which sitteth upon the throne, and unto the Lamb." Verse 10. Now let's continue reading:

"And all the angels stood round about the throne, and about the elders and the four beasts, and fell before the throne on their faces, and worshipped God, Saying, Amen: Blessing, and glory, and wisdom, and thanksgiving, and honour, and power, and might, be unto our God for ever and ever. Amen. And one of the elders answered, saying unto me, What are these which are arrayed in white robes? and whence came they? And I said unto him, Sir, thou knowest. And he said to me, These are they which came out of great tribulation, and have washed their robes, and made them white in the blood of the Lamb. Therefore are they before the throne of God, and serve him day and night in his temple: and he that sitteth on the throne shall dwell among them. They shall hunger no more, neither thirst any more; neither shall the sun light on them, nor any heat. For the Lamb which is in the midst of the throne shall feed them, and shall lead them unto living fountains of waters: and God shall wipe away all tears from their eyes." Verses 11-17.

John, the beloved disciple, banished to the isle of Patmos,

is the one who holds this conversation with the heavenly beings. It's encouraging to see that John was prompted to ask about the great multitude and then received the answer. The dialogue is almost humorous. The elder asks John, "Who are these, and where did they come from?"

And John replies, in essence, "How should I know?"

Then the explanation is given, after John's attention has been focused in the right place. "These are they which came out of great tribulation, and have washed their robes, and made them white in the blood of the Lamb." It's good news, isn't it—robes get white when washed in red!

But if you look ahead to the beginning of the very next chapter, there is silence in heaven. What does that represent? First you see this great multitude, then silence in heaven. Christ is returning, and heaven is empty and silent while He makes the trip to bring His loved ones home.

So it's obvious that the 144,000 and the great multitude appear on the scene at the time of the very end.

There is one major comment on this passage of Scripture that we should read for help to a better understanding of these verses. It's in the book *The Great Controversy*, pages 648 and 649.

"Upon the crystal sea before the throne, that sea of glass as it were mingled with fire—so resplendent is it with the glory of God—are gathered the company that have 'gotten the victory over the beast, and over his image, and over his mark, and over the number of his name.' "

When does the mark of the beast appear? It appears in Revelation 13, remember? Has anyone received the mark of the beast yet? No. There are people who are preparing to receive it, but no one has received it yet. The mark of the beast is given after there has been a decree made that you either receive the mark of the beast or risk being killed. So the group of people being described here in *The Great Controversy* are the ones who live after the time of that decree.

Let's continue: "With the Lamb upon Mount Zion, 'having the harps of God,' they stand, the hundred and forty and four thousand that were redeemed from among men; and there is heard, as the sound of many waters, and as the sound of a great thunder, 'the voice of harpers harping with their harps.' And they sing 'a new song' before the throne, a song which no man can learn save the hundred and forty and four thousand. It is the song of Moses and the Lamb—a song of deliverance. None but the hundred and forty-four thousand can learn that song; for it is the song of their experience—an experience such as no other company has ever had. 'These are they which follow the Lamb whithersoever He goeth.' These, having been translated from the earth, from among the living, are counted as 'the first fruits unto God and to the Lamb.' Revelation 15:2, 3; 14:1-5. 'These are they which came out of great tribulation;' they have passed through the time of trouble such as never was since there was a nation; they have endured the anguish of the time of Jacob's trouble; they have stood without an intercessor through the final out-pouring of God's judgments. But they have been delivered, for they have 'washed their robes, and made them white in the blood of the Lamb.' 'In their mouth was found no guile: for they are without fault' before God. 'Therefore are they before the throne of God, and serve Him day and night in His temple: and He that sitteth on the throne shall dwell among them.' They have seen the earth wasted with famine and pestilence, the sun having power to scorch men with great heat, and they themselves have endured suffering, hunger, and thirst. But 'they shall hunger no more, neither thirst any more; neither shall the sun light on them, nor any heat. For the Lamb which is in the midst of the throne shall feed them, and shall lead them unto living fountains of waters: and God shall wipe away all tears from their eyes.' Revelation 7:14-17."

So this group of 144,000 have passed through the time of trouble, through the outpouring of God's judgments, the seven last plagues. Here again, it is evident that these are the people of God who are alive just before Jesus comes again in power and glory.

Both the 144,000 and the great multitude which no man can number come forth out of great tribulation. Both are alive at the time of Christ's return. Both have been washed and made white in the blood of the Lamb.

Probably the most asked question in connection with this study is a question of concern about the number 144,000. Is it a literal number? Is it a figurative number? Could it perhaps represent heads of families, instead of individuals? The news of a great multitude which no man can number brings hope to more hearts, doesn't it? But if that great multitude is brought in from outside the remnant church, then that hope is for the ones out there, not for those of us already within the church!

It's sort of like worrying about the size of the ark at the time of the Flood. Have you ever been in on a discussion on that one? What if 8,000 people, instead of only 8, had repented and decided to enter into the ark. There wouldn't have been room! What in the world would God have done then? Would some truly repentant souls have been left outside? Would the Flood have been canceled?

Abraham had a similar question when he talked with God under the oaks at Mamre, regarding the fate of Sodom. Abraham was worried that God didn't know His business and that some who were righteous would be destroyed along with the wicked. Abraham finally settled for ten, and God agreed not to destroy the city for the sake of ten, if such could be found. But the God who does not destroy the righteous with the wicked found only three. And they weren't exceptionally righteous, were they? But the three were spared, even though the city was destroyed.

We can rest in what we have been told, that it is our choice, not the choice of God, as to who can be a part of the 144,000. There will be no one who genuinely seeks to be a part of that group who will be excluded or told that all of the seats are already taken.

If all who are prepared will be included, then the most important aspect would be to find out what are the characteristics of the 144,000 and what is necessary to be among that group.

Let's look again at the chapter in *Early Writings* on the shaking. In Revelation 3, there are three groups of people up until just shortly before Jesus comes. They are the hot, the cold, and the lukewarm. But by the time of Jesus' return, the lukewarm have disappeared. They have all gone either hot or cold. What causes this is the shaking, but it is simply a term for the polarization which will take place, when people go one way or the other.

According to the chapter on the shaking, this happens inside of the church, and on the outside of the church as well. Those in the church who have been lukewarm go one way or the other, either hot or cold. Then those who are cold leave the church, and only those who are hot are left. When that happens, the power of God and His Spirit can be poured out in fullest measure, and the final message to the world will go at tremendous speed.

Those who leave the church during the time of the shaking will be replaced by those coming in from the outside who have accepted the message of the three angels under the power of the latter rain.

Let's summarize, then, the characteristics of the 144,000.

1. They have a special experience such as no other group in the history of the universe. Notice that it is a group experience. There may have been individuals here and there who have had such an experience, but this is the first time an entire group or company of people have had it.

2. They have gained the victory over the beast and his image and his mark. That pinpoints them in time.

3. They have stood without an intercessor through the final outpouring of God's judgments.

4. They have seen the earth wasted with famine and pestilence and the sun having power to scorch men with great heat, obviously the seven last plagues.

5. They have passed through the great time of trouble.

6. They have experienced the time of Jacob's trouble.

7. They are translated from among the living. They are among the few from among men never to taste death.

8. They are the first fruits unto God and unto the Lamb, and if they are the first fruits, then there is this great multitude that no one can number that follows.

But there is something even more important than the characteristics of the 144,000, and that is their character. From the passages in the Bible and *The Great Controversy* just considered, these points seem to be self-evident.

1. The 144,000 receive the seal of the living God. What is the seal of God? It is the Sabbath, the commandment within the ten where the elements of a seal are found. But what does the Sabbath represent? Rest. Rest from your own labors, and allowing God to do what only He can do. The Sabbath is also a sign of sanctification, right? It's more than just a day on which to go to church. It's a sign of a relationship with God that has resulted in total dependence upon Him.

2. The 144,000 have a pure religion. They are doctrinally pure. There may be those outside of the remnant church who understand a genuine relationship with God, but who do not have the understanding of the truth when it comes to doctrine. Those who are among the 144,000 have both the experience and the pure doctrine.

3. The 144,000 have obtained the complete victory. They have no guile; they are without fault. They are the same on the inside as they are on the outside. There is no deceit involved in their lives. They have obtained not only the victory over their behavior, but God has complete control of their hearts and minds as well.

4. They have an experience with God that did not come

easily. They were willing to agonize in prayer, to persist in seeking God, even when everything looked dark.

If you want to be among the 144,000, if you want to obtain the victory they receive, then there is only one way to accomplish it. Real victory is getting the victory over trying to get the victory! Real victory comes in realizing that whatever victory is necessary, is totally God's work, and none of ours. Our part is ever, always, and only to come to Him for fellowship and communion, accepting of the gifts He has to offer. Those who follow the Lamb whithersoever He goeth in heaven are going to be those who made following Him first priority in their lives while on earth.

The 144,000 are so intent on following the Lamb, so determined to stay with Jesus Christ and allow His control in their lives, that they will be willing to die, rather than to worship the beast and his image. They will have come to the place where the worship of God is their top interest, their primary concern. They love not their lives, even unto death. They are willing to give up even their temporary existence here in order to continue the relationship of faith and trust in Jesus and accepting His righteousness in their behalf.

Would you be willing to give up your own life rather than to accept a system of righteousness by works? When the crisis comes, will you be ready to choose fellowship with Christ over any other consideration? How can you know?

The true test comes to each person on a daily basis. Did you give up your own life today and give God top priority, in spite of whatever else clamored for attention? Were you willing to give up your plans and accept His plans for you for today? Did you spend time with Him, regardless of what other changes it required you to make in your schedule? If you are not choosing Him day by day now, in the time of peace, there is little chance you will choose Him when the crisis comes. But as you place Him first in your life each day, He will give you grace to continue to place Him first, one day at a time, until the day you see Him face to face.

Chapter 8
The Times of Trouble

Medical science has made many breakthroughs in recent years, and the women's liberation movement has accomplished many of its goals. But the last I heard, none of them have managed to arrange it so that men can have babies. Men can follow their wives into the labor and delivery rooms of some hospitals and watch the entire birth process. But it ends right there. It's still the women who give birth to the children.

If a man were to discover that he was going to have a baby, it would be an astonishing thing, wouldn't it? And the Bible uses the analogy of a man giving birth to make a point about the times just ahead of us. We'll read that verse of Scripture in just a minute.

Bear in mind then, that there will be three times of trouble. This is a topic that has been quite familiar to our subculture, and it is as biblical as your Bible. We cannot talk about last-day events without getting into the subject of the time of trouble, or rather, the times of trouble.

You may remember from the first chapter of this book that we were told a long time ago that the time of trouble is going to be worse in reality than in anticipation. That's just the opposite of many of our trials and troubles in this world. Often we find something is not as bad as we had anticipated. But we're told right up front that in the case of the time of

71

trouble, the real thing will be even worse than the description. And many of us have heard things like this since the time we were boys and girls. Some people I've heard of lie awake at night worrying about the time of trouble. Sometimes we have erred, as parents and teachers and preachers, in not telling about the resources that will be available to us during that time, so that instead of feeling frightened, we can face it with courage. That's part of our purpose in this chapter.

But let's take some time to look at the information we have been given concerning the times of trouble and what we can expect from God during those times.

Continue to bear in mind that there are three times of trouble. One of them, before the close of probation, is referred to as the "little" time of trouble, sometimes called the early time of trouble. There follows, after the close of probation, "A time of trouble such as never was," and along with that one is another, called "the time of Jacob's trouble."

Well, let's take a brief look at the little time of trouble. In the information available, the reason it is called "little" is that it is of short duration. It is a time of trouble that comes to the 144,000, those who remain after the shaking time. As they go out with great power and the earth is lightened with the glory of God, the wicked are enraged—particularly the religious wicked—and as a result there is a time of persecution. The persecution will be severe. During that time before probation closes, some of God's people will even lose their lives. There will be martyrs, as in the Dark Ages. So in one sense, we may wonder why this could be called a "little" time of trouble. It sounds pretty big! But it is little in duration, and it is even little in its impact upon God's people, for Jesus said, Don't fear those who can kill the body, but who cannot kill the soul.

So we can take refuge in the remembrance of the martyrs who, though burned at the stake, died singing hymns of praise. There is nothing to fear, for even though they got the bodies of Huss and Jerome, they never even came close to their souls.

And there's something else that we have been told concerning the little time of trouble, in case anyone is fearful. We are told that the courage and fortitude of the martyrs is not even supplied until it is needed. If this is true, then it is pointless to spend time talking about the persecutions and stress of the time of the martyrs, because doing so will inevitably wipe you out. If we were to try to describe in detail some of the persecutions of the Dark Ages, with extra bolstering from modern inventions and ways of torturing people, we could all lie awake for many nights, and with good reason. For we would not have the courage to face any of it, since that courage is not supplied until it is needed. For that reason, we will go over the little time of trouble rather quickly and go on to something more important.

Let's consider the great time of trouble, which comes after the close of probation. You'll find it mentioned in Daniel 12:1. "At that time shall Michael stand up." Who is Michael? Christ. "The great prince which standeth for the children of thy people." Here is an insight we don't want to miss!

We have had a real fear grip us in the past because we have gotten the idea that there comes a time when Michael stands up, probation is closed, and we no longer have an intercessor. We'll look a little longer at that in the next chapter. But Hebrews says that Christ is the one who "ever liveth to make intercession" for us. Hebrews 7:25. So there will never be a time when we have to live without an Intercessor. There apparently *will* be a time when we will live without an Intercessor for the *forgiveness of sins*, because the power of God will have led us to complete victory over sins. But we will never be asked to live without an Intercessor in terms of power available to keep us from falling—and that's one of the roles of an Intercessor! Intercession and mediation have two purposes: One, since we are not big enough to forgive our own sins, we need an Intercessor to plead our case for forgiveness. Two, we're not big enough to live without sinning, and we need the power that comes through the intercession of Christ. We are told that even the unfallen worlds are preserved from falling through Christ's mediation and intercession.

So when it says here that Michael stands up, we need to realize what that means. He's not going to leave us! He is going to stand up for His children.

Go back with me to a day when a man was dragged outside of Jerusalem. His face shown like the face of an angel. And as they threw rocks at him, he looked up, the heavens were open, and what did he see? He saw Jesus standing. Standing at the right hand of God. Jesus was not going to take this sitting down! He stood up in behalf of Stephen. And this verse in Daniel 12 tells me that Jesus is going to stand up for us too. He will stand "for the children of thy people." Isn't that good news?

Then it says, "There shall be a time of trouble, such as never was since there was a nation even to that same time: and at that time thy people shall be delivered, every one that shall be found written in the book." What is this time of trouble, such as never was? You read about it in both Daniel and Revelation, and it is the time when the seven last plagues are poured out, and the whole earth is in chaos.

Is it a time of trouble to be afraid of, as far as God's people are concerned? Yes or no? Of course not! If you've read Psalm 91 lately, then you know there is nothing to be afraid of. "There shall no evil befall thee, neither shall any plague come nigh thy dwelling." Verse 10. This time of trouble that is worse in reality than in anticipation is for the wicked. Who are the wicked? There might be some Seventh-day Adventists among them, isn't that right? Just because you are a Seventh-day Adventist today doesn't insure that you won't be among the wicked. The wicked are those who do not depend upon Christ for their hope of salvation. And these have everything to fear. The wicked, who try to live their spotless lives apart from Christ, have everything to fear during this great time of trouble. The wicked are those who have time for everything else except personal fellowship with Christ day by day; for the worst thing anyone can do is to live apart from Jesus. Are we clear on that? It is the one who lives apart from Christ who is wicked. The wicked maintain the separation from God, while the righteous maintain the connection with God. There's the difference. So let's stop defining wickedness merely in terms of doing bad things.

Some young people have gotten the idea that the way to escape the time of trouble is to break off relations with God before that time comes, in order to escape persecution. But the truth of the matter is that the time of trouble will be the worst for those who are without God and without a shelter. It will be a time of trouble for the whole earth. And while those who are under the shadow of the Almighty are sustained through His power and are promised that bread shall be given them and their water shall be sure, there is no promise of protection for the wicked. During the time that the seven last plagues are being poured out, the ones who have everything to fear are the ones who are living apart from God. God's children are safe in His hands.

But let's go on to the third time of trouble, the time that is called Jacob's trouble. Jeremiah 30, beginning with verse 3, has an application for this time. "Lo, the days come, saith the Lord, that I will bring again the captivity of my people Israel and Judah, saith the Lord: and I will cause them to return to the land that I gave to their fathers, and they shall possess it."

The first interpretation of this passage would be for literal Israel and their return to Jerusalem from their Babylonian captivity. But what would be the interpretation for those of us who are Christ's, and therefore Abraham's seed? What is the land of our fathers? Who was the father of the race? Adam. And where was the land in which Adam and Eve worked and lived? The Garden of Eden. The Garden of

Eden is in heaven today. But we have been given the promise that we can return to that land, haven't we? So there is a double application here. We have also been promised that we will be able to return to the land of our fathers.

Verses 4-6. "These are the words that the Lord spake concerning Israel and concerning Judah. For thus saith the Lord; We have heard a voice of trembling, of fear, and not of peace. Ask ye now, and see whether a man doth travail with child? wherefore do I see every man with his hands on his loins, as a woman in travail, and all faces are turned into paleness?" Modern illustrators might depict the situation as a man is standing with his hands on his abdomen, his face is pale. Well, I would think so! Of all things, God uses this kind of analogy to show what terror and what consternation would come concerning this particular time that is being described.

Verse 7. "Alas! for that day is great, so that none is like it: it is even the time of Jacob's trouble; but he shall be saved out of it." So this time of Jacob's trouble is what causes people to turn pale and is the event which God uses such an amazing illustration to try to describe.

What was Jacob's trouble? Let's go back now to the record in Genesis 32:24-31. Get out *Patriarchs and Prophets* and read the chapter entitled "The Night of Wrestling." It's the story of Jacob and the angel.

But here, let's read the Scripture record of that night. "Jacob was left alone; and there wrestled a man with him until the breaking of the day. And when he saw that he prevailed not against him, he touched the hollow of his thigh; and the hollow of Jacob's thigh was out of joint, and he wrestled with him. And he said, Let me go, for the day breaketh. And he said, I will not let thee go, except thou bless me. And he said unto him, What is thy name? And he said, Jacob. And he said, Thy name shall be called no more Jacob, but Israel: for as a prince thou hast power with God and with men, and hast prevailed. And Jacob asked him, and said, Tell me, I pray thee, thy name. And he said, Wherefore is it that thou dost ask after my name? And he blessed him there. And Jacob called the name of the place Peniel: for I have seen God face to face, and my life is preserved. And as he passed over Penuel, the sun rose upon him, and he halted upon his thigh." He was lame, he was crippled. In fact, Jacob was crippled for the rest of his life.

Back in camp, when Jacob was seen approaching the next morning, someone said, "Who is that coming?"

"That's Jacob."

"No, that's not Jacob. That man is limping."

"Yes, he's limping because he's been with God."

"You don't limp when you've been with God, do you?"— but the truth is, sometimes you do!

Well, what happened that night? Jacob got in a fight with Jesus! Have you ever been in a fight with Jesus? It sounds terrible, doesn't it? But Jacob had been fighting Jesus all of his life.

Jacob's fighting with Jesus was the real reason that brought him to that very brook on that particular night. He was there because he had been exiled for years; and in the process he had been separated from his home and family, and his mother had died. He never saw her again after they conspired together to gain the birthright by fraud. He had been a stranger in a strange country, and it was because of his great sin that he feared his brother was coming to take his life.

What was his sin? Well, we might say his sin was lying in order to obtain the birthright. But the reason for the lie was that Jacob had tried to accomplish by his own efforts what God had promised to do for him. That had been his pattern all of his life. "God helps those who help themselves" had been his motto. You see, God has this terrible habit of waiting until the last minute to fulfill His promises. Have you discovered that? God had promised Jacob the birthright. Then God waited and waited, clear up until the day and hour that Esau was out collecting the venison to bring home to receive the birthright. And still God waited!

Jacob and his mother Rebecca got their heads together and said, God has finally bitten off more than He can chew. We'd better help Him out. After all, God helps those who help themselves!

Jacob had a granddaddy who had the same kind of problem. He also had a grandmother who made the same mistake. Remember Abraham and Sarah? God had promised them a baby, but He waited until she was ninety years old! Even in those days, ninety years old was definitely senior citizen age. If Sarah had had a baby at that point, it would have been paid for by Medicare! No doubt about it. Nobody on the geriatric wing is in there for childbirth. So, long before her ninetieth birthday, Sarah had come up with a clever arrangement. She and Abraham, with a little help from Hagar, were able to produce a baby. But it was the wrong baby. It was the child of their own efforts, and not the child of faith. The whole issue for Abraham and Sarah, and for Jacob and Rebecca, was to accept that what God has promised to do, He will do. He does not need our help—in fact, when we try to help, we only get in His way.

For Jacob's entire life, in spite of the fact that he was a converted man, in spite of the fact that he had morning and evening worship—and there were little piles of stones all over the land to prove it—he still had been involved in a desperate struggle, trying to learn that what God has promised, He is able to perform.

Right up to that very night, Jacob had continued his efforts in his own behalf. His strategy was clever—the Pentagon would have been pleased. He had divided his company into two groups, so that if one group was attacked, the other might escape. That way, he would save at least 50 percent. He even went a step further and made sure that the group that appeared to have the best chances of survival was the group that included his favorite wife, Rachel.

He had sent some servants ahead of his groups, with sheep and cattle to appease his brother Esau, just in case a bribe or peace offering would make a difference.

And *finally*—as a last resort—he went by the brook and began to pray. He had it backward, didn't he?

Then he felt that heavy hand on his shoulder. He resisted it. His first fear was the fear that he was going to die. He struggled for his life. He was afraid he was going to be killed.

Then a second fear came, as the struggle continued. The second fear was the kind that comes from guilt and remorse. He became afraid that he was in this situation because of his own sin. That he was reaping the results of his own actions. He was afraid it was his fault. He felt the pressure of guilt that, had he been faithful, it would never have come to this.

And we are given this story as an illustration of what God's people are going to go through during the time of Jacob's trouble, just before Jesus comes again. We can notice several lessons by similarity—and a couple by contrast. But let's continue.

During the "time of trouble, such as never was" (Daniel 12:1), when the world is in chaos and the seven last plagues are being poured out, the wicked of the world are going to decide that there is a reason for this. They will reason as have heathen villages in the dark parts of the world of yesteryear. Maybe you remember hearing how they dealt with calamities. Trouble would break out in the village. It might be drought or disease or whatever. The witch doctor would go through his mumbo jumbo and come up with a victim—someone who was responsible for all the trouble. Then the villagers would deal with the one thought to be responsible so that the gods would be appeased.

At the very end of time, the same thing will take place throughout the world. As the time of trouble, such as never was, breaks upon the world, the religious wicked (who have always been the most wicked of all the wicked) begin to look around to find out who's responsible. They point to a group of people who are known for their loyalty to the Creator. And they decide: "If we could get rid of these from off the face of the earth, then the trouble will be over." So they begin a campaign against God's people.

In the process, God's people begin to have real stress. No question about it. They go through a major crisis. One of the first things that happens is that they are afraid they are going to be killed, that they are going to suffer and lose their lives. But this is quickly replaced by deeper fears. Their second fear is the same as Jacob's. They are afraid that it is their own sins that are responsible for bringing them to the impasse at which they find themselves.

Note this description found in *The Great Controversy*, pages 618 and 619: "As Satan influenced Esau to march against Jacob, so he will stir up the wicked to destroy God's people in the time of trouble. And as he accused Jacob, he will urge his accusations against the people of God. . . . He has an accurate knowledge of the sins which he has tempted them to commit, and he presents these before God in the most exaggerated light, representing this people to be just as deserving as himself of exclusion from the favor of God. . . . As Satan accuses the people of God on account of their sins, the Lord permits him to try them to the uttermost."

You can forget about the little time of trouble, before probation closes. You can forget about the big time of trouble, such as never was. But this one, you can remember. And when it comes to you, maybe you'll remember some of the things we are considering here.

"As Satan accuses the people of God on account of their sins, the Lord permits him to try them to the uttermost. Their confidence in God, their faith and firmness, will be severely tested. As they review the past, their hopes sink; for in their whole lives they can see little good. They are fully conscious of their weakness and unworthiness."

These are not people who have gone around talking about

perfection, and boasting that they have finally gotten the victory over pride and haven't sinned in three years. These people are fully conscious of their own weakness and unworthiness.

"Satan endeavors to terrify them with the thought that their cases are hopeless, that the stain of their defilement will never be washed away. He hopes so to destroy their faith that they will yield to his temptations and turn from their allegiance to God." He wants to come in with such blackness and heaviness of spirit that they will say, "Oh, I guess I never was really a Christian anyway; best to forget the whole business, curse God, and die." That's what Satan is trying to get them to do.

These people are tortured, as was Jacob, with their past sins. They are reminded of all the times they have depended upon themselves, instead of depending upon God. And God allows Satan to try them to the uttermost. In fact, we are told that "alarm and despair will seize them, for it appears to them as to Jacob in his distress, that God himself has become an avenging enemy."—*Signs of the Times*, November 27, 1879.

Then comes something that teaches us a lesson by contrast, rather than by comparison. Jacob was by the brook Jabbok that night largely because of a concern for his family. Now this does not mean that we are not going to be concerned about our families and loved ones during the time of Jacob's trouble. But this will be one time when each individual will be at the brook Jabbok for himself. There won't be certain representatives down by the brook, while the rest of the family are back in camp, sleeping. Everyone will be by the brook. That's one difference. Nobody is going to slide through the time of Jacob's trouble on someone else's coattails. God has no grandsons and no granddaughters—only sons and daughters.

Let's return to Jacob and his experience as an illustration of God's people during the time of Jacob's trouble. There is something else here that we may have missed. We have had the idea, and I think I am speaking correctly for most of my subculture, that the reason for the struggle in the time of Jacob's trouble is that we are afraid for our lives, afraid of being tortured or killed. We have even added the fear that our sins have not been forgiven and that we will be lost eternally as a result.

But there is another greater fear which is not so self-centered. It's found in the final paragraph from the book *The Great Controversy*, page 619: "Though God's people will be surrounded by enemies who are bent upon their destruction, yet the anguish which they suffer is not a dread of persecution for the truth's sake; they fear that every sin has not been repented of, and that through some fault in themselves they will fail to realize the fulfillment of the Saviour's promise: I 'will keep thee from the hour of temptation, which shall come upon the world.' Revelation 3:10. If they could have the assurance of pardon they would not shrink from torture or death." So they are not so much worried about torture or death, but whether they have the assurance of pardon. But notice the reason they are worried.

"If they could have the assurance of pardon they would not shrink from torture or death; but should they prove unworthy, and lose their lives because of their own defects of character, then God's holy name would be reproached."

These people are concerned for God, not for themselves. That proves the kind of people God has led them to become. Their greatest concern is that God's name will be dishonored. They have come to a stature in their walk with God that Moses demonstrated so long ago, when he said, "Leave my name out of the book of life, just save these people."—for whose sake? For God's sake. That *His* name not be reproached by the heathen.

For Jacob, and for the people involved in Jacob's struggle, the wrestling continued until the victory was obtained. Jacob said, "I will not let you go unless you bless me." His faith took hold upon God and the righteousness that was greater than his own, and he refused to give up the struggle until the blessing was realized.

As the people of God pray that prayer, God is going to stop them. He is going to say to them, "You don't have to worry about letting go of me before I bless you—because *I* will not let you go until I bless you."

There's a song that says, "Lean on me, when you have no strength to stand. When you think you're going under, hold tighter to My hand." But the responsibility for our salvation does not rest with us, even in the last great struggle with evil. When we have held onto His hand as tightly as we know how and it's still not enough—we have the assurance that *He* will not let go until He blesses us. He will never let go, so long as we want Him in our lives. The love that will not let us go will be sufficient to see us through, even during the time of Jacob's trouble, and we will be saved out of it.

Then the people who have gone through Jacob's trouble will stand up straight and tall and hold their heads high, as in the distance they see a cloud approaching. Suddenly all of the angels of heaven will be in attendance, and the heavens will be on fire, ablaze with the glory of God. Their troubles are over for all eternity. What a story! What a hope! What a future!

Chapter 9
Without an Intercessor

There is no such thing as operating with a battery-powered Christian life. It is impossible to store up ahead the power needed to take you through to a time when no power is available. The Christian life has always been based on the trolley-car principle. You are either in touch with the power source, or you're not. Either you're alive, or you're dead. And that principle is not going to change after the close of probation.

There is no evidence that we are going to be forsaken by God or by the Holy Spirit or by the angels during the times of trouble. We have been given some information on the role of Christ as Intercessor during our final days here on this earth, but we need to look at it more closely in order to understand it correctly.

Let's begin, however, with our Bible base. First of all, Isaiah 53:12. It's talking about Jesus, and the last verse of the chapter says, "Therefore will I divide him a portion with the great, and he shall divide the spoil with the strong; because he hath poured out his soul unto death: and he was numbered with the transgressors; and he bare the sin of many, and made intercession for the transgressors." It's good news that through Christ we have an Intercessor for transgressors, isn't it?

Then there is Romans 8:26, where we find the Holy Spirit

in the role of Intercessor. "The Spirit also helpeth our infirmities: for we know not what we should pray for as we ought: but the Spirit itself maketh intercession for us with groanings which cannot be uttered." So the Holy Spirit intercedes for us concerning our infirmities and concerning our prayer life. And that's good to know.

Next, we have the well-known text in Hebrews 7:25, a key text, speaking of Jesus. "He is able also to save them to the uttermost that come unto God by him, seeing he . . ." intercedes for us until the close of probation? What does it say? "Seeing he ever liveth to make intercession" for us. That's a good clue to some of us who thought we were going to be left to work out our salvation on our own.

And in this connection, just to underline the fact that we are never left on our own, at any time, let's read Romans 8:38, 39, even though the word *intercessor* is not used. "I am persuaded, that neither death, nor life, nor angels, nor principalities, nor powers, nor things present, nor things to come, nor height, nor depth, nor any other creature, shall be able to separate us from the love of God, which is in Christ Jesus our Lord." Paul really pulled out all the stops, listing all of the conditions he could imagine and assuring us that God will never separate from us so long as we choose Him. The only thing that can ever cause us to be separated from God is if we choose that separation.

And finally, we noticed in Daniel 12:1 that Michael stands up "for the children of thy people." It doesn't say He leaves them, but He stands up for them, because He's on our side. This "standing up" has ordinarily been associated with the close of probation. But when He stands up, it is not for the purpose of leaving His people on their own.

So what does it mean to be without an Intercessor, after the close of probation? Before we try to draw some conclusions, let's notice a couple of quotations from the gift to the remnant church. The first is found in *Signs of the Times*, February 14, 1900. "Christ is . . . the High Priest of the church, and He has a work to do which no other can perform. By His grace He is able to keep every man from transgression." So the work of keeping from transgression is part of His work as what? As High Priest.

Then, in Manuscript 73, 1893: "It is as necessary that Christ should keep us by His intercessions as that He should redeem us by His blood. Those purchased by His blood He now keeps by His intercession."

So there are two reasons for an Intercessor. First, because we need pardon for our sins and our sinning, and second, because we need power to overcome. Do you see both of them mentioned? Christ is involved in His intercession for pardon and for power. He is Intercessor for justification and for sanctification, if you please. Remember those two things.

Now the plot thickens. In *The Great Controversy*, page 489, we read, "The intercession of Christ in man's behalf in the sanctuary above is as essential to the plan of salvation as was His death upon the cross. By His death He began that work which after His resurrection He ascended to complete in heaven. We must by faith enter within the veil."

So the intercession of Christ involves His death, as well as a continuing work He carries on in heaven—and keep in mind that both pardon and power are involved here.

Here's another insight. "Christ is mediating in behalf of man, and the order of unseen worlds also is preserved by His mediatorial work."—*Messages to Young People*, p. 254. As our Mediator, or Intercessor, Christ has two functions— to pardon and to empower. The worlds that have never fallen are kept by His intercession. They are not strong enough to keep from falling in their own strength. They need His power, even though they have never needed His forgiveness. Adam wasn't strong enough to keep from falling. He separated from the Source of power. And that's been our problem ever since.

Now when Michael stands up, when we are shown the scenes of Christ's leaving the sanctuary, throwing down the censer, and we live during a certain period of time without an Intercessor, the evidence is that He will have brought us by His grace to a point where we will no longer need an Intercessor for forgiveness of sins, since we will have been given the victory. But *we will always and forever need His intercession for keeping power.* In fact, the reason we will no longer need His intercession for sinning is that we will have discovered His intercession for keeping power.

Hebrews 7:25 doesn't say that He ever liveth to make intercession for sinning—it says He ever liveth to make intercession for *us.* And that will never cease, throughout eternity. Isn't that right?

So even though there is a sense in which we will live for a period of time without an Intercessor for sinning, we don't need to fear that we will be left to continue overcoming on our own power. His mediatorial and intercessory work to keep us from sinning will continue unbroken.

So the challenge to God's people everywhere is not to try to discover how to force themselves to be obedient, so that they will somehow get a strong enough "habit" of obedience so as to "make it through" the time when Christ's intercession for sins has ceased. The challenge is to discover how to depend upon Christ's keeping power day by day, moment by moment, so that we will learn now the lesson of trust in Him and the danger of trusting in ourselves and our own strength.

How do we learn to trust in Him instead of ourselves? Once again—there is only one thing *we* can do. We trust the One we know to be trustworthy. As we spend time with Him, day by day, in communion and fellowship, through His Word and through prayer, we get acquainted with Him. The trust then comes as a result of that acquaintance. So the bottom line in preparation for the events of the last days is the same as the bottom line for living the Christian life today. Do you know Him? It is in knowing Him that we find life eternal.

The Chart

If you would like to read the most concise and helpful chapter that some of us have found, describing the sequence of last-day events, try the chapter entitled "The Shaking" in the book *Early Writings*, pages 269-273!

The following chart is based primarily on that chapter, as well as on an excerpt from the book *The Great Controversy*, pages 618, 619.

The chart begins during the time of the Laodicean church of Revelation 3, when there are three groups: The hot, the cold, and the lukewarm. During the time of the shaking, which some of us believe is taking place at this present time, the middle group of lukewarm people disappears, as those who were previously lukewarm go one way or the other.

Following the shaking time, those who have become cold leave the ranks of the remnant church, while those who are on fire for God go forth under the power of the latter rain to give the loud cry message. Those who are cold receive the mark of the beast, while those who are hot are given the seal of God.

As the message goes like fire in the stubble and thousands accept the truth about the three angels and come to join the ranks of the remnant church, persecution begins. After all have had an opportunity to receive or reject the message, probation closes.

During the time after the close of probation, the seven last plagues fall upon the wicked, while the righteous are brought through the time of Jacob's trouble. At the close of that time, God's people are delivered, and Jesus comes to take His people home.

Won't you accept the challenge today of continuing to seek the relationship with Him, so that you will be ready to accept your role in the closing drama?

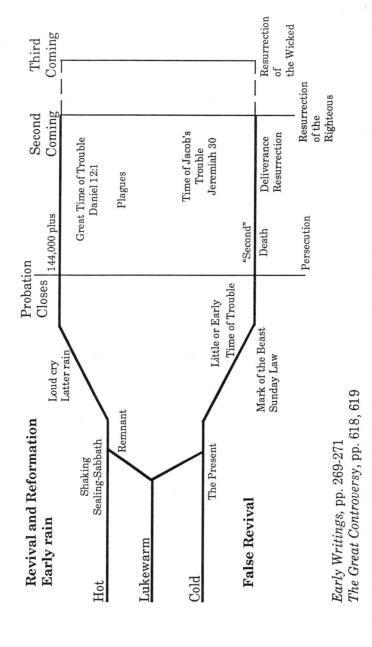

LAST-DAY EVENTS

Early Writings, pp. 269-271
The Great Controversy, pp. 618, 619